The River of Forgetting

The River of Forgetting

A Memoir of Healing from Sexual Abuse

by

Jane Rowan

Booksmyth Press
Shelburne Falls, MA

Published by Booksmyth Press
102 Mechanic Street
Shelburne Falls, MA 01370

Parts of the Introduction and Chapter 32 were published as "Unintended Consequences" in *Women Reinvented: True Stories of Empowerment and Change,* LaChance Publishing, Brooklyn, NY, 2010.

Chapter 16, "Out-Raged," was first published in *Seeking Out Light Newsletter #3,* Guilford, CT, 2008.

Cover photograph from Jane Rowan's family files.
Cover Design by Maureen Moore of Booksmyth Press

ISBN: 978-0-9815830-2-0

LCCN: 2010909295

Dedication

To all the survivors of painful childhoods
and to the caring therapists who
help us heal.

Contents

Lost

The River

Moving On

Heading for the Light

≈ Prologue: Rivers of Detail, Oceans of Fog

IT'S ONE OF THE GOOD memories.

My father is bending over the hull of the upturned boat, picking out the old caulking, scraping away at last year's paint and barnacles. He uses a putty knife to push ropes of smelly, tarry oakum into the cracks. He will paint the boat gray, with a rusty fouling-resistant paint on the underwater part to keep the barnacles from slowing it down.

The fierce sweating sun is trapped on the oyster-shell shore between the steep bank and the water, making an island of heat. My father wears cut-off pants and one of those ribbed cotton undershirts with the thin straps. His shoulder muscles bunch and his freckled skin is red. He has a cap to protect his balding scalp, or else he has tied a handkerchief at the corners to make a rough covering. He swears occasionally when the knife slips.

I come near him and poke at the soft blisters of gray paint. I can only stand the heat for a short while, but I scrape until my eight-year-old arms get tired. Then I walk out onto the wooden dock to watch the tide come in and the little fishes swim.

The sun-bleached scene is clear: the brown leather sandals I have to wear against the sharp oyster shells, the scarred wooden sawhorses holding up the boat, the strands of brown seaweed doodling the high tide mark, even the nails in the cedar posts of the dock. Hours of pleasure and idleness.

I HAVE OTHER MEMORIES, blurred in a sickly fog. Urgent night voices behind closed doors. "What can we do about it?" "There's nothing we can do." "She's too young to remember; she'll be all right." And memories murkier still, fastened into my spine and pelvis with binding force, huge with emotion, no pictures.

When the foggy memories arrived, they rocked my world, forcing me to ask dizzying questions: What is truth and how do I know it? Is it in the Kodak-sharp image? In the wrenching gut, the nausea? How do I keep the clear-cut detail and also give the nebulous shadow its weight, neither denying the other?

This is the story of how the past overtook me, how I found help, and how at last I integrated the shadows of my childhood into my life. In the process, I found unexpected love, joy, and freedom.

To My Sisters and Brothers

Little blue eyes looking up from the oyster shells,
crispy pencils of reeds beached and dried,
my father laboring hotly over the hull of the boat,
all perfectly clear.

What are the details of a fog?
Memories that had to go far away,
stripped down, fragmented.
Unwanted sensations, but no place
no pattern of the wallpaper
no light. No feeling of the rest of my body,
if I have one,
no person doing this to me.

Dizziness pulls my body backward in a spiral.
This fog is my fog
this lack of detail is the tale I must tell.

Others have wandered the same landscape.
At the edge of the downward spiral path
is a hut where pilgrims may rest.
I see their footprints in the dust.
And I know I have built this labyrinth,
I have called back the little girl who leads me there.
I told her, I believe you, I am listening
so she could speak, though her speech had no words.

When these words make our scenery appear,
it is a magic we are doing
writing our life into existence.
It is an offering to the others,
our sisters in the fog.

≈ Introduction: Unintended Consequences

I DIDN'T INTEND TO become a writer or an artist. I didn't intend to grab at an early retirement offer and leave teaching, a job that I loved. I certainly didn't intend to find out about childhood incest.

These days I spend my mornings writing poetry or fiction, or painting abstract canvases. Those days, I got up hurriedly, checked my to-do lists, grabbed my briefbag already loaded with student papers and lecture notes, and headed off to the office.

I would not have moved from there to here without the raging crisis in the middle. It began with an unsolicited memory from age three. After the first memory came, I wrestled with doubt about whether anything at all had happened to me as a child.

I DIDN'T INTEND TO spend several years immersed in the waters of my psyche, but my emotions left me no choice. My lifelines were my therapist, my friends, and my creative outlets. My therapist taught me to listen to the voice of the little girl inside me who had been molested and who felt intensely abandoned by both parents.

Currents of ancient emotions swept through me. In therapy and in my daily life, I crawled through thickets of mistrust and bogs of shame. I was enraged at people who trampled my boundaries. And yet I functioned well at work and kept up friendships. Slowly, my focus shifted away from the misery and need of the child inside me. As I began to trust my therapist's love and acceptance, I gained a sense of being a sturdy, worthy person who had already survived the worst.

I wouldn't have called it creativity at first. I simply needed to write in my journal every day, keeping track of my feelings as they swirled. I'd sit at the kitchen table and let my pen race uncensored.

But words were limiting, too. When I was abused at ages three to six, I didn't have words for what happened. Fifty years later I needed to involve the wordless, unscientific parts of my mind in the work of recovery.

I took up pastels and scribbled dark, angry pages full of red and black. And I took my body-memories and reactions to the dance studio to act them out.

OTHER PEOPLE HAVE WRITTEN moving stories of childhood abuse, detailing the trauma of their early years. Although I have plenty of childhood memories, I do not have clear recollections of the abuse, only fragments and body memories. It's the adult experience of healing, with all its human messiness, that is the core of this memoir. Because it focuses on self-discovery, love, and creativity, I hope this book will also be useful to many individuals with differing backgrounds who undertake the inner journey of self-knowledge.

I am still my mother's daughter—the persistence and discipline, the stubbornness. I am still my father's daughter—the quest for something more, dashing off on new projects, the inventiveness. But I am my own daughter as well, the beloved creative child.

THIS IS THE STORY of my transformation.

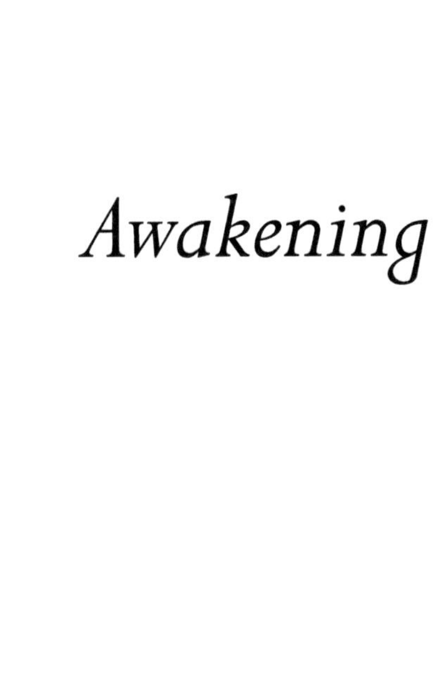

Awakening

≈ 1 Pandora's Box

THE MEMORY EMERGED from a dim corner of my mind, jolting me awake. It was a humid morning in August. The air flowed softly through the bedroom window, bringing in a catbird's song from the cherry tree just outside. I sat up in bed and propped a pillow behind me, grabbed my spiral-bound journal from its place on the bedside table, and began scribbling:

> *I am three or four and I hurt between my legs. I'm perched on the toilet in the big bathroom in our house at Shell Beach. The door is opposite me and the light streams in from the window on my right.*
>
> *I feel the sting when I pee. My mother says that I slipped in the bathtub and fell on the bathtub rim. I have no memory of anything that caused the hurt, but I know I don't believe her story of how it happened.*

Fear sank claws into my stomach. I wondered what had happened and who had hurt me.

No way. Surely not. Not my father. I don't know how to tell what's true. I don't want to make things up.

THIS WAS REVELATION DAY, the day that started me on a long journey into my past. How did it happen that a 52-year-old woman suddenly woke up to the possibility of long-ago abuse? What had kept the issues at bay so long? Why could the past now grab me by the throat?

At that point I had been divorced for ten years, after a long marriage. I had a college-age son, several good friends, and stable family ties. My father had died a year previously at the age of eighty-three, after a long illness with Parkinson's disease. My elderly mother lived alone about two hours away from my home.

I WAS A SCIENTIST. Evidence was my bread and butter. Even though I'd moved on from laboratory research to administration, there was nothing I liked better than a juicy set of numbers. Scientific arguments could be fierce and competitive, but they were based on demonstrable facts. I didn't yet realize there was knowledge more important than facts.

I taught organic chemistry at a liberal arts college and was successful in my work. I loved the give-and-take of classroom teaching as well as the opportunity to guide individual students' lives. Department politics were more difficult. I had just been passed over for the position of department chair.

It was an odd process. After the faculty met to discuss the candidates, it was clear that a younger man and I were the top choices.

Two women faculty were the steering committee for the process. One of them, Rebecca, pulled me into her office and closed the door. "We have some concerns about you as chair," she said.

I planted my feet on the floor and prepared for the punch.

"You're too pushy. Harry and some others said that if you were chair, they'd have to get their grades in on time."

"This is a problem?"

"You come on too strong in a bunch of ways; that's just one. Now, if you could write a memo to everyone in the department to let them know that you recognize your problem and you promise to soften, I think you'd have a good chance."

"No, I'm not going to do that."

I didn't get the position. The public Jane was plenty assertive about ideas and principles, but I slowly came to know parts of myself that were frightened and quiet.

THE PEOPLE WHO WEREN'T at the party were as important as the ones who were. The smell of broiling bluefish filled the kitchen and dining room of my mother Myra's modest home that July day, a month before my revelation. My sister Kathy bustled around the kitchen, my mother stood in the doorway to the dining room with her hands on her hips, Kathy's husband and my son sat around in the living room, while I finished setting the table. The sounds of traffic filtered in through the window screens and lingered like dust on the family silver a hundred years old, sterling remnants of my father's old Baltimore ancestors. My family was small, just my parents and their three daughters. Grandparents, aunts, and cousins had always been distant, both geographically and emotionally.

My mother, whose birthday we were celebrating, was 82 that year, her back hunched, her hair streaming back gray from her lined, pleasant face with its oversized glasses. She would have been bustling like my sister, except she was not allowed to do that on her celebration day, so she stood and watched us be busy, reminding us of any detail we overlooked.

Absent, of course, was the father whose great-grandfather's portrait was on the wall, whose Uncle Matthew's chairs were pulled up around the family table. He had last been seen here five years ago, trembling and pale-faced with Parkinson's, the disease robbing him of his expressions and his words. The first anniversary of his death fell the day after my mother's birthday, but we would not talk about that.

I'd always been on good terms with my parents. I visited them about once a month as my father aged and became incapacitated. Finally a fall and a broken hip sent him to the nursing home, which was both unfortunate and a great relief. My mother, a tiny woman, had been taking care of everything, including helping him in and out of bed, doing all the cooking and cleaning, and all his personal care. After his accident I continued to travel down to visit both of them, wheeling him out of his dim room at the smelly nursing home and outside to the patio whenever possible.

He never came back to the house in the four years between his fall and his death.

My older sister Suzie was also not at the party. She had been pushed out of the nest at age three because of her Down syndrome. Back in the 1940s, of course, virtually no one kept a Mongolian idiot at home. She was sent away to a special private school in upstate New York where a woman with a cushiony bosom mothered all of her thirty retarded chicks with impartially warm regard. Now Suzie lived twenty minutes away in a foster home. She watched TV and did needlepoint, was proud of her work at a sheltered workshop. And yet each time my mother's birthday came around, Mother said, "Oh, let's not invite Suzie. It's too complicated."

Finally the dinner was ready and we called in my son, Will, and Kathy's husband, Richard, from the living room. It was a bit awkward figuring out who would sit at the head of the table where my father had always sat, even though he hadn't been there for five years. My mother settled it with a directive—"Kathy, why don't you sit there and serve?"—rather than mention his absence. Kathy, Richard, and I made trivial conversation during dinner while Myra and my son were characteristically quiet.

The next day I was alone with my mother. We did not converse much, but she gave me many chores to do. In the few months surrounding my father's death, she had been open to talking about him, but now when I asked something about how she was feeling without him, she said, "Oh, I don't like to think about that. I'm fine."

IT TOOK ME A LONG TIME to understand the importance of the sister who wasn't there. As I grew up on the sidewalks and in the scrubby backyards of my Connecticut neighborhood, the kids asked, "Don't you have any brothers and sisters?" Most of them were from sizable Catholic families.

"No, I don't," I said awkwardly, thinking of my sister Suzie and my family's trips to see her in the summer. Kathy was not born until I was fifteen, so I grew up like an only child. When I started school my mother told me, "When kids ask, just tell them you don't have any brothers or sisters. It's a lot easier than explaining that she's retarded and she doesn't live with us."

In fifth grade I told my best friend about Suzie. We had a pact that she wouldn't tell on me and I wouldn't mention her wearing glasses. One day in a pique I called her a "four-eyed dinosaur." In retaliation she told the other kids, "Jane's sister is a retard," and they teased me. I challenged her to a fistfight, my one and only fight in elementary school, and bloodied her nose for telling my secret.

All through my growing-up I saw Suzie about once a year, on our trips to the school in the bucolic village where the Down syndrome kids played on swings and talked in their strange slurred accent. The school taught them the basics of reading and writing—a stunning innovation for the 1940s. When this wonderful school changed hands, my parents brought Suzie back to Connecticut to be cared for within the state system. My mother said proudly that Suzie was queen of the roost at the state institution for the few weeks she was there, before she was placed in a foster home.

I thought that Suzie was just a tiny part of my life, a distant figure to be taken for granted. Then one spring day in 1991 I walked into a local card shop to pick out a birthday card to send to Suzie. Under the fluorescent lights, I stepped sideways to browse the birthday cards. *To my sister, for all the memories we've shared.* Nope. *My dear sister—the giggles, the tears, the hopes, the fears.* Not true for us. *Sis, my best friend, my companion.* No, no, and no! To my surprise I felt tears of frustration welling up—I had a sister who was not a sister. I chose a generic card from the kid section to send.

I brought my distress to Sarah the next day. She was the therapist I'd been seeing for two years at that point and the one who would guide me through so many years of work. She had an office on the main street of my small town. I entered and shut the door on the traffic sounds. As I waited, I scanned the familiar objects in the room. Her many educational certificates and diplomas were framed on the wall, along with photographs of trees and a sketch of a woman holding a child. A large wooden bookshelf held the psychology books she freely lent to her clients, a collection ranging from Gestalt therapy to family dynamics books to popular self-help. I noticed a new rock crystal, smoky yellow, on the table next to her chair. Her new-age stuff was just a little outside my comfort zone.

Sarah walked in wearing her usual garb—loose, colorful rayon pants and a soft shirt. She was a slender woman about my age with graying wavy hair and alert brown eyes. After we greeted one another, I told Sarah how I'd felt at the card store.

"Of course, she's your sister."

"But I don't remember a thing about her. She was only three when she was sent away."

"How old were you?"

"Two. Really, too young to remember."

Sarah made a note on her yellow pad, then looked at me with sadness in her eyes. "But just the right age to suffer from a separation. Can you recall any feelings about her?"

"When she was little, not even a glimpse. Mostly I remember the trips to see her in upstate New York, every summer. We'd drive up through the Catskills and have a couple days of vacation on the way. Then we'd visit her at the school."

"How did you feel when you saw her?"

"I didn't feel much, it seemed like. But now...." I reached for the Kleenex and wiped away some tears.

"Are you willing to try something?"

"What kind of thing?"

"I think some contact with your younger self could be really helpful here."

"I don't know." She could probably hear the skepticism in my voice. "I can't remember anything from that time."

"Sometimes we remember more than we think we do, when we let it come bit by bit. It helps to do a little light hypnosis, if you are willing."

"OK, I'll give it a shot." I had always been curious about hypnosis.

"Get comfortable," she said. I shifted a little in my chair. "Now just breathe. One, getting relaxed... two, going deeper inside."

Voices in my head said *This is hokey. Why am I doing this?* I noticed a cloudy feeling of relaxation. A quiet space opened up inside my mind, while my thoughts still circulated.

"Now let your mind go back to an early time in your childhood. Can you remember some place clearly?"

I remembered back through my teen years of social embarrassments, academic successes, school friends. Junior high, classroom scenes and buses. Grade school and the house by the river. "Yes, I can see my room in the house where I'm maybe seven years old. There is my bed by the window on the wall that faces the street, a chenille bedspread, the Venetian blinds. The big wooden phonograph player and the cabinet with the 78 rpm records." It was clear in my mind, even though it shifted a little, as the furniture had probably been shifted around.

"Can you feel yourself in that place?"

"Yes, it feels real." I floated through the familiar rooms of my childhood.

"Good. Now see if you can go back further in time."

"It's shadowy."

"Don't worry, just breathe and let it come. See if you can get any feeling from the time that Suzie was there."

"I can't... it's... no pictures. It's long before grade school. We must have been living in New Jersey but I don't see...." I spoke slowly from a dream state. I had a vague sense of large grownups moving around a sofa in a room.

"Let anything come...."

"I just have this feeling of hugging someone. A solid soft body right here...." I placed my hands on my stomach and chest. The sensation of warm pressure was comforting and familiar. I started to cry. Sarah made a slight, encouraging sound.

"I think I... she... she was *there*. That's what I remember, someone to hug." I sniffled and reached for another Kleenex. "They took her *away*! My sister!"

"It's true. You were little and they took her away."

"Oh, I miss her! She never came back." After a few minutes I sighed and opened my eyes, finding my way back to the solidity of Sarah's office, glancing out the window at the budding trees. I had been far away.

"Suzie was a comfort," I said. "She was my big sister."

"I think you loved her a lot. I think it was very hard when she was taken away."

"But they had to do it."

"Probably they needed to, but it doesn't mean that you had to like it."

"And they didn't want me to be sad about it. Somehow I know that. My mother especially. She was sad herself but she didn't know how to comfort me. She tried to make me cheer up. I was only two!"

"Just when you needed their help. That's exactly how the child learns not to have feelings. It's how a young part of you gets split off."

"What's that?"

"The little one who is not allowed to have those feelings becomes kind of stuck back there. The purpose of the inner child work is to get in touch with her and bring her back into your life."

The experience felt powerful, but I didn't know whether to trust it. It certainly wasn't like science, where everyone could see the evidence.

I WAS THINKING OF QUITTING therapy, that summer before Revelation Day. In the previous several years I'd worked with my feelings about Suzie and other family patterns, and I thought I'd had enough. I was doing fine. Work was all right despite its ups and downs. Friends and family were steady.

On a sticky day in July I entered Sarah's office, which was now in the basement of her house. I sat there on the clunky but comfortable tweed couch, waiting for her to come in and looking out into the jungly green back yard. She was late, as usual. I arrived promptly and as I waited, I wished she'd show her caring by coming on time. This day I was nervous because I had told her I might want to end. I wondered whether I had to tell her that I hadn't been feeling close to her lately. I was afraid to challenge her, to risk the fragile thread that seemed to connect us.

Sarah walked in with a folder of notes and said hello. She settled in her customary chair, offered me a glass of water, and took a sip from her tea. She looked at me both keenly and sympathetically. It was that combination of quick intelligence and warmth that had attracted me to her as a therapist. "When you started with me in 1989, it was about four years after your divorce. The divorce itself didn't seem to be on your mind that much. You came in with distress about some conflicts at work, I remember."

"Yeah, that's true."

"You said right away that you didn't want me to hassle you about relationships—do you remember?"

"I do remember. Some of my friends were on my case about finding a lover and I didn't want a therapist bugging me, too."

"Well, I certainly don't want to push you about finding a partner or anything like that, but how do you feel about the kinds of support and intimacy you have in your life? Does it feel like enough to you?"

I admitted that I did not feel enough intimacy in my life, not enough close friends. I wished I could be closer to my mother and my much-younger sister Kathy, but was rebuffed when I tried to talk about emotions. I had to acknowledge that relationships were a problem area, worth working on. I didn't talk about my reservations about Sarah, because her attentiveness that day reassured me. I was back on board, committed to more therapy, not knowing that the boat was headed for the rapids.

PANDORA'S BOX—that was the image that plagued me as I thought about relationships. In the fairy tale as I remember it, the young girl Pandora is shown a little box and told she must never open it. One day, while the grownups are away, she of course opens the box. All manner of evil things fly out of the box and into the world: Pestilence, War, Poverty, and Meanness. Last of all, Hope flies out to keep humans going.

The moral of the tale, in Hawthorne's version that I read as a child, is that little girls need to obey and not mess with closed boxes. Later I did some library research and found that the original Pandora may have been an all-giving and very powerful goddess, who was later tamed and relegated to the role of naughty girl.

I was furious that the grownups blamed Pandora for all the evils in the world. Meanwhile, they had created the setup to lure her into "wrongdoing." I wrote in my journal:

> *Pandora. They left her all alone, and in her loneliness she opened that box. When they came back, they knew from the ugliness that came into the world that she, all by herself, alone and only, had opened that box.*
>
> *And I? What is in the box for me? I am so bad that people pull away from me, they flee. Am I shut up in the box for this? Everyone is right to be scared of me, no wonder they keep me in a box.*
>
> *Before she opened the box, they say, there were no troubles in the world, no lies, no sharp teeth, no sorrow. And they expect me to believe that, that this fully grown world, with castles and mysterious chests, had no troubles, no pain, no deceit? Oh no, they blamed it on her, but they had put the box there. They knew all about it. It makes me feel dizzy.*

And what has this to do with intimacy? With my feeling of hideous wrongness? I must be the contents of the box, I must be the girl to blame.

A few days before Revelation Day, I was sitting across from Sarah and wondering where to start when she asked, "How do you feel now about working on relationships?"

"I'm scared." I looked down. "I don't understand. I didn't have a bad childhood. I should be able to love and attract people."

"Uh-huh."

"What's *wrong* with me?" I asked her. I was surprised at the intensity of the fear that knotted my stomach.

"Can you reframe that and defuse it a bit?" She leaned forward and looked concerned. "You're being hard on yourself."

"I can't. That's the way it really feels. Putting other words on it won't make it feel different. I feel like I'm bad and it makes me lonely."

"Why don't you go back in time and see if the little girl inside can tell you about her feelings?"

"OK." I sighed.

"Just breathe and let your attention settle in deeper. Go back as far as you wish."

I could see my grade-school self back inside the dim rooms of the big house by the river. "I feel sad and angry. I know I'm not supposed to feel this way."

"Anything more?"

"Nothing much is coming. I still just feel *wrong* and *bad*, that there's something wrong with me."

"Just let things come."

I caught a fleeting image of sitting on the toilet in the bathroom in our earlier house. It seemed trivial so I let it pass by without saying anything. Then I felt dizzy as a cloud took over my consciousness. My eyes were closed and I spoke from a distance. "Sarah, I feel the fog again. It is red and huge."

Feelings of blurriness had been coming up for a while, intense sensations of dizziness and disorientation. I was blinded by gray or colored fog. Sometimes in therapy I felt lost for long periods of time. Later, Sarah used the word "dissociation" to describe my state. Over time I began to notice fog creeping in when I would get close to something that my defenses did not want me to know.

In that session where Sarah invited my inner child to help us with the question of relationships, nothing much seemed to happen. There was the blur, and three days later, the revelation.

≈ 2 Couldn't Be

I DUG OUT OLD PICTURES. Could this be me, the same girl in the black-and-white photographs? The girl in the Girl Scout uniform, with the long braids. The first-grader in the school picture wearing the cotton dress with puffy sleeves, looking solemn—could she have been molested, abused? It was true that I didn't smile in the pictures, but surely what I remembered was a normal childhood.

Surely my father, *my own father,* could not have been doing nasty, dirty things to me. And if he did, where was my mother?

IN HER QUIET OFFICE, my therapist Sarah listened to my incoherent story, my false starts on sentences, the things blurted out. "I remembered this time... I know I was three or four because we only lived in that house for a short while. I'm sitting on the toilet and it hurts when I pee. It stings. I know it is supposed to be that I slipped on the bathtub over there and hurt myself on the rim, but that isn't true. It's not!" My shoulders and stomach were tight as I struggled to speak.

"Do you remember any more details about the scene?" Her brown eyes watched me gently.

"The bathroom was upstairs at the top of the stairs. Opposite the toilet was the big bathtub with feet. The door was left of the bathtub."

"Anything more?"

"After I was finished going to the bathroom, my mother would wash me with boric acid to take away the sting. Somehow I remember that's what it was called, 'boric acid.'" I remembered the cool sensation of the washcloth between my legs.

"But I don't remember anybody doing anything to me," I wailed, feeling scared.

"Do you have any sense who it might have been?" she asked.

"No, not really. But it feels like it had to be my father. But I don't know! I don't know, it's all really vague except that memory about peeing. How do I know if it's real?"

"People don't make these things up for fun," she said. I took a deep breath and sighed. I was somehow afraid I was making it up to get her attention.

"I feel so sad. Why am I sad? I just want to cry and cry."

"It's all right to cry. I'm here."

And I did. Even though I didn't yet believe my memory, I began mourning for the relationships I thought I had, the ones I wanted and needed, the safe mother and father. I mourned for the picture of a family that I had carried all this time, a normal-enough family to raise a normal-enough person. If this picture was false, who was I now? Was I now crazy, a victim, a non-functional, abnormal person? Because of my sister Suzie's Down syndrome, the question of normalcy in my family was heightened (although unspoken), and it was ironic because my parents also aspired, like other intellectuals, to being different from "ordinary people."

"You'll probably feel tired," Sarah warned me as she hugged me goodbye. "This is hard work." I was comforted by the contact and the concern I heard.

Sarah was careful, then and always, not to lead me or suggest anything to me about what might or might not have happened. Her restraint let me trust that whatever came up was mine, not hers. I had enough doubts all on my own without having to wonder if she had planted ideas in me. And at that time, there were numerous stories and allegations in the press about "false memories." Parents and other people accused of abuse were counter-attacking and claiming that suppressed childhood memories were fiction. I wrestled with doubt every day.

Tiredness. This realization is like an infection to be fought with my whole body.

After waking this morning I think nah, impossible. And then yeah, that's what they always say. I must realize I am traumatized—it feels like a death or something. Trauma. Shock.

Besides the overwhelming emotions of sadness, confusion, and later, anger, physical sensations intruded on me. Any time I thought about the suspected abuse, I got an ache in my lower belly, right above my pubic bone. I started noticing that this ache was there a lot of the time, even when I was not consciously thinking about the abuse. The ache became so constant that I asked my doctor to run a urine check to make sure I did not have a bladder infection. I didn't.

A few days after Revelation Day, I called my friend Marianne. She was also a teacher at the college, but in literature, so that I had few professional contacts with her. She was a short woman but a formidable presence, a consummate professional in her field and a feisty woman who was engaged in local politics. I had met her in a women's group twenty years earlier. She'd later quit the group while I remained.

In addition to being my closest friend, Marianne had told me about child sexual abuse within her family, so I knew she would take me seriously.

"Marianne, I had a memory come up..." I paced the kitchen floor, clutching the phone.

"Tell me," she said in her direct manner.

"It was when I was three or four. I can remember being in the upstairs bathroom and it hurt when I peed." I told her the basics.

She did not press for details. "If you find it's true, that's really stunning."

"But I'm not sure of anything."

"That's OK. I'm sure it will come. Please take care of yourself. You know you can call me any time of day or night."

I sagged against the doorframe, tears of relief tracking down my cheeks. But soon I had to finish packing my suitcase and drive to the airport. I had been invited to give a talk on curriculum reform at a good liberal arts college in the Midwest.

At the time of the revelation, it was summer break, but I was drafting a major grant, one that would support the work of almost every member of the chemistry department. I was incredibly busy with professional work. I look back on it now and wonder how I kept up the pace, and why.

I checked into the motel and unpacked. Before dinner I pulled out my little spiral-bound notebook and sat in a comfortable chair to do free-writing. I kept the ball-point pen moving, letting words flow without censorship, not trying to make sense. Anger and sadness washed through me. The important thing was to give space, not logic, to the feelings. After twenty minutes I stopped to read back over the scribblings, then put the book away. I put on a dressy jacket and my professional persona, locked my room and walked across campus to meet my hosts and talk about education.

SOLITUDE! I NEEDED some time alone where I could sort out my feelings. After the Midwest trip and before the semester began, I took a week's solo retreat. The setting was rustic with small wooden cabins where solitary people were expected and respected. My first instinct, when looking for safety, was to be alone. It took a long time to imagine that I could look to others for help.

I struggled simply to believe myself. I filled spiral-bound journals with daily attempts to understand.

> *It seems these memories, whatever they are, are not very available. It seems they are well buried. Carefully protected.*
>
> *If it really was Jack (my father) and really with Myra's complicity, that could be hidden pretty carefully—the child had no one else at all, no one to help, no one to turn to, no one to believe her. The two central—and only—people, so what could I do except try very hard to pretend nothing happened?*
>
> *If this is true. And I'm still of two minds. One mind still saying, "Yeah right. You're making it up." The other saying, "Mmm. This is too real not to be true. This memory has been hanging out and flapping at you for a while."*

I needed time and space to work with the memories while I was on retreat, but how? I was lucky to have creative resources: I wrote, drew, and danced. Each of these was just for myself. It was important to me that others not see and judge, especially my crude drawings, although I often showed them to Sarah.

My retreat cabin was one spacious room with bare wood floor and glorious windows on three sides looking out into woods and more woods. It had two gas burners for cooking, and I hauled water in jugs each day from the well about a quarter mile away. No electricity, no hum of appliances, just the sigh of the wind in the trees, birdsong and squirrels. One morning I set aside an hour in which to write, draw, or move as the mood struck me. I slowly stretched on the floor, letting feelings be with me and letting them guide my movements. Suddenly I wanted to use oil pastels,

> *exploding into drawing of slash slash anger—red, black, yellow, chaotic and urgent. NO! anger slash. No clarity of focus or images just NO NO anger NO ... tears, so beautiful.*

There was no target of the anger, no people in the drawings, just the raw feeling. The anger gave way to tears that washed me clean for the moment and I drew diagonals of soft gray-blue-green, peaceful.

All that week, I walked and meditated, drew and wrote, loving the quiet of the woods and the solitude. Every day I observed my feelings recircling around the same themes of shock, grief, anger, and disbelief. One morning I had an especially vivid dream:

> *It looks like an incredibly tiny black child, naked sitting there. Oh my—somebody has to do something for this child. No one else did—I guess it's up to me. So I go close and it's even tinier, it is so small. I take it up and it clings to my finger as tiny as a tree frog—I think yes, a newborn will do that. I pick it up gently and then it has turned into a furry brown animal—it's, I should know what it is—it's a bush baby.*
>
> *So I'm the right one to take care of this little one. I should know. I take it home and look in the fridge. All the while I know I'm late for something, some meeting or whatever. In the fridge—I'd like to find milk and bread or fruit. I see some fruitcake or raisin bread and pick out a bit of that. Nothing much really good for it. Can't find any milk.*

Some part of my unconscious knew that I had just begun a long process of growing the secret up into my life and learning how to take care of my hurt, young self. While the conscious self wanted quick breakthroughs and "progress," a wiser self knew that the new work was absolutely tiny and frail, needing every care.

> *The Big Bad Secret seems as distant as ever or maybe more so. I wish for some breakthrough, with all its pain. But I look and I see—if this is really it, then this child has a hell of a lot to deal with. We moved a lot when I was very young. No other part of the family was close. There were no big people in my life other than my parents. No siblings. Suzie was gone and Kathy was not born until I was fifteen.*
>
> *This child had no one to rely on except those who may have betrayed her. No one, no one, no one at all. She can't afford to give up this secret easily. It means redefining everything. Everything.*

A FEW WEEKS AFTER my solo retreat, my women's group met at my house. I had been a faithful member for seventeen years, while the membership changed slowly. The group had started as a consciousness-raising group, and we shared many revelations about our lives, women's lives. All the gendered things that made us feel "crazy"—power, sex, relationships, work situations—had been shared, laughed about, and cried over. The group had been a mainstay for me during my divorce ten years earlier, but lately I had been feeling a bit alienated. We usually spent a lot of time on individual "check-ins," but seldom got into depth on personal issues.

This evening, I greeted each of the women at the door with a hug. The six of us congregated in my kitchen to make tea. Then we seated ourselves on the two sofas and assorted chairs in the living room. I grew tense as I listened to other people's news and waited for the circle to get around to me. The things on my mind felt murky and I was very hesitant to voice them.

"I've been having some disturbing memories from when I was three or four." I fell silent and glanced up to see each woman looking intently at me.

My mouth was trying to form grown-up words to say, "I was sexually abused," "molested," "fondled." I found I did not know how to choose the words; they weren't in my everyday vocabulary. And those words were woefully inadequate to begin to describe my experience of the memory and its fallout.

At the same time, I felt like a little girl inside—distressed and completely inarticulate. This part of me had no words at all for what had happened. She was overwhelmed at the prospect of telling and wondered if she would be believed. I sat there with shame and confusion rising in my body until they reached my heart, my throat, my mouth, and my brain. This thing that had happened to me felt dirty and secret. I was sure that the shame covered my skin, smearing me with ugly bruised colors. If I told the secret, then people would see me as ugly and dirty, too. I would lose my standing as an adult and become a child-victim—pitied, scorned, weak, and shunned. I would lose the protections I had worked so hard to build and retain. I took a breath and started again.

"I think I was molested. It's really unclear what happened, I really don't know. I think it was my father. I'm working on it in therapy."

At this time when I intensely needed affirmation, needed people to tell me, "I believe you. You're not crazy, whatever it is that is coming up," I did not yet have the vocabulary or the confidence to ask for help. Nor did my friends know how to respond. Some women shifted in their chairs, while others were stock-still. Someone said, "That sounds hard," but no one else said anything. I felt lonely and unsatisfied.

"You stop that this minute!" Pam yelled at the group of four or five boys. The setting was idyllic, a beach at a state park in the hills with a sparkling lake rimmed by dark forest, white sand, and only about fifty people sitting or swimming. I was there with Pam one day in that summer before my revelation. She was a quick-witted, quick-tempered woman in her late forties, full of anecdotes and stories. We'd been good friends off and on for fifteen years.

Pam's six-year-old daughter was there with a five-year-old friend. The friend was somewhat dark skinned, and a group of eight-year-olds began teasing her, calling her ugly. Pam marched right over and chewed them out, "What gives you the right to talk

You ask

Remember when you
were a child, who
made you feel safe?
I cannot name a one.

There was no appearance of danger.
    Dreams
of fierce foxes approaching
but no knives pointed at me.
    Nights
when things happened
not to be spoken at all.
    Things
not named but known.
So I could not speak
could not be safe.
My small soul wandered
alone in the gray fog

So I grew up successfully
but without my soul
to rejoice with,
to cry, to dance on the sand,
to reach for another's hand,
to sit inside me and be glad.

It's a long return to find
the soul that went away.
A long return
to speak her back
call her back
earn her trust
hold her lightly
caress her hair
feel her trembling now
as she speaks.

to her like that? How would you feel if someone called you ugly and a group of people picked on you? You quit it and keep away!"

I saw Pam protecting the child from insult, marching up to her tormentors and confronting them. I cannot imagine it. I thought kids were supposed to ignore such things. It never occurred to me that they could be protected like that. Never.

The passivity, the urge to hunker down and hope I'll be passed over, the fear, the frozenness, the expectation that I am helpless and all I can do is wait and hope it won't hurt too much and maybe they won't notice me next time. And not exactly that I deserve it, but why shouldn't they do that to a kid? No concept of the right to be protected. No way.

THAT FALL I WAS SWEPT away by the busyness and excitement of teaching. In the evenings I talked constantly on the phone, organizing part of a charity event in my town. I was trying to pull together the big grant before the deadline. I also flew out of town to conduct more faculty workshops.

It felt impossible to find enough time for all the feelings that inhabited my soul and body. To relieve some of the pressure, I set aside twenty minutes every morning before work. I sat in my favorite rocking chair in the spacious light of my living room, closed my eyes, and turned my attention inward.

Sometimes a wave of feeling—neediness or grief or wrongness—washed over me. I stayed inside the emotion, letting it shower me, and some understanding might come. As I sat with a sudden feeling of wrongness, I might recall an incident at work and see how a student's plea to see me right away triggered old feelings that I must please everyone.

If no feeling pounced on me, I would try to ask my inner child what was happening with her. In these early months, she was like an adopted real child, shy and untrusting. The adult part of me tried to be patient and reassuring, learning how to become trustworthy. Sometimes there were mere glimpses of a girl running by or hiding from me. Most of the time I knew she arrived when I felt a rush of sadness and tears.

I've been so busy, suddenly I feel so sad. Ancient sadness. No end. It feels like a raisin shriveled up in my chest where my heart should be. I want the red hot pain of opening and living, loving people and things, loving the world as it is. Instead I have this shriveled little triangle.

I want to cry but I can't. The tears swim at the edge of my eyes. Little girl, I want to hold you and let you cry.

THE ENTRANCE OF THIS MEMORY into my life, with the suggestions it raised, left me staggering and blinded in a snowstorm of emotions. I did not know how to relate to family, to friends (To tell or not? When? How?), to the world, to my past. I did not know whether to believe my small voice, my young self. I did not know anyone who had had a similar revelation, or thought I didn't. I had no idea how long the work would take. I kept wanting things to move along and get clearer on a timetable of weeks or months, when in fact it took years and it was not a matter of getting clear in the same way I expected.

I told Sarah that I was anxious about what would happen next and how soon. She said, as she would say to me many, many times, "It takes a while. You really have to go slow and respect the child's needs."

I got teary. "What is happening now?" she asked, leaning forward.

I said, "It's the little girl. She's fearful and anxious. How can she even begin to tell this story—to doubt the old story, with no new story to replace it? Nothing is clear. You have to be really brave to say, 'but I know it didn't happen the way the grownups say...' and not know the next part."

"That's true," she said.

"And I'm terrified of saying bad things about my family. What if I'm wrong and none of it is true?"

"Just take it slowly. It will become clearer in time."

The doubt created a torturous double bind. If I really had been abused by my father, then I was afraid I was a victim—stigmatized and not credible. I heard accusing voices: "How could you say such a thing about your family? How do you know that?" On the other hand, when I did not believe myself, I felt crazy, because those painful feelings had no cause and no attachment.

I remember taking a walk with another friend, Brenda. She knew something had happened and asked kindly and logically, "When did it happen? How old were you?"

"Sometime before I was five, I don't know exactly."

"How long did it go on? Did he keep doing it?"

"I don't know." I started feeling panicky because I couldn't answer her questions. How could such an important memory be stored with no age or place? I understand now that many of our memories, especially childhood ones, are poorly anchored. How many times have you attempted to place an event—"When did I first see the Statue of Liberty? Well, I was in Girl Scouts, so I must have been ten at least. I think I wore the green uniform, or was it Brownies and the brown one?" As adults, we usually have enough markers in our lives that we can place things by associating them with particular other memories that we revisit.

The other reason for lack of detail is that different types of memories get laid down in different ways, as brain research is now showing. There is evidence that memories acquired along with massive doses of stress hormones are indeed more fragmented and different in quality from normal memories. In particular, fear associations get stored in the amygdala, a primitive, quick-response part of the brain where memories are vague, associative, and emotional. Thus, the triggers for fear responses can be rather general and not "logical." An area called the hippocampus helps consolidate concrete "declarative" memories. But the hippocampus is suppressed by stress hormones. So the more tangible details of memory can be lost during stress. In addition to these distortions of the original memory processes, shameful abuse memories are not revisited and rehearsed—rather, they are shunned—so they do not get anchored to other dates and events.

I wanted to be able to answer Brenda's simple queries about time and place. When I could not, I felt I was not credible, so I became afraid to tell people.

I had a little crying girl inside me all the time.

I entered Sarah's office feeling more nervous than usual. I sat down to wait, worrying over the possibilities and impossibilities I had been pondering.

Alone at home in the evenings, I had spent more time trying to bring back memories. I desperately wanted to know what had happened. However, as I asked my younger self to tell me more, I only heard disembodied voices. I was in a dark place with words drifting past me. A male voice said, "It's not like she was raped."

I also heard, "She's too young to remember. She doesn't understand."

But that afternoon I didn't tell Sarah about the voices. Instead I squirmed on the sofa before I said, "I keep worrying over these questions."

"What questions?" she asked. "You can raise them here. It's OK."

"I don't understand. If he really raped me, wouldn't there have been some changes in my body?"

I glanced at Sarah for reassurance. She looked straight into my eyes. "Go ahead, say more."

"I mean, when I first had sex when I was in college, there was blood. Doesn't that mean I was a virgin? Is that possible if he raped me?"

"I'm not sure. But tell me—did it have to be rape with his penis?"

"But that's the kind that *counts*."

"No, that's not the only kind that counts. If he used his fingers, that is serious, too. He was still violating you."

I didn't believe her—it didn't seem real and serious if he "only" used his fingers.

I think I had overheard hushed conversations when I was a child, in which my father said to my mother, "It's not like she was raped." Being so young, I would not even have known what the word meant, but I learned that what he did was not important, that there was some weightier act called "rape," which did *not* happen to me.

IN DAY-TO-DAY LIFE, I felt awash in feelings. The next time I saw Sarah, I told her I couldn't only be dealing with my child-self. "I'm afraid the little-girl feelings are going to take over. I want you to remember I am a grownup, too."

"I know that, and you are a very strong and competent grownup."

"Then why are we always dealing with the child? Sometimes it makes me feel crazy."

"The child parts of you are the parts that have been suppressed; they need extra care and attention. But I will keep in mind your adult self—I know it's important."

I felt a bit reassured, but also frustrated—always this child-stuff! It was hard to stay with it while I needed to go about my business in the world. I wanted to feel more whole and less wholly childish.

All my long-held beliefs about family were in question. Was my feeling of wrongness in the world really the result of abuse, or just the human condition?

Surely I'd had a normal childhood. My parents were eccentric—I knew that and cherished it. But I pondered the quality of their care as well as the myths and patterns that held us together. Could this family possibly have supported abuse?

≈ 3 Family Snapshots

MY FAMILY DID NOT KEEP photo albums. All the photographs, old and recent, were jumbled together in a drawer in an antique secretary desk. Occasionally someone would write a name and date on the back of one of them.

Black and White

IN THIS PHOTO MY FATHER is in his early thirties, with thinning hair, holding a toddler in coveralls—that's me—in the crook of his arm and a gray and white kitten in the same hand. The little girl has short bobbed hair and her smiling mouth is open. Her chubby right hand is waving in the air near his face. He's leaning back, grinning, playfully putting his other hand up to dodge the girl's open hand. Their two bodies seem utterly comfortable with one another.

In this picture, he's alone, a little older, leaning against a chain link fence with a cigarette dangling out of his mouth. He looks tough in a 1950s kind of way, his closed mouth stretched in a grin, eyes squinting at the sun. In back of the fence is a worksite with a blank paved area.

At this age he was already mostly bald, the light glancing off the planes of his head. He was wearing a leather jacket. Was it the jacket, the hands jammed into the pockets or, more likely, the tilt of the shoulders that said, "defiant"? Perhaps the cigarette had a lot to do with it, dangling no-hands from his lower lip.

The smoke snaked upward towards his eyes, which were crinkled at the corners. James Dean without the looks or the hair.

But he was attractive in fact. A man interested in everything. He had a boyish enthusiasm for squirrels, snakes, bats, and boats. He did not hesitate to walk through back yards in strange neighborhoods or to speak to the brakeman in the railroad yard where he was trespassing. He wrote impassioned notes in the margins of books, disagreed with Republicans and bigots, belonged to the ACLU, was proud of his Confederate ancestors, fought prejudice and unthinking patriotism, and employed talented outcasts in his shop.

Jack was a man of contradictions, with his boundless curiosity, his sullen moods; the momma's boy who never learned to pick up his own black cotton socks, the patient teacher, the one of rages.

Sarah once said, "Of course, what child wouldn't be attracted to him, with his childish enthusiasms? He sounds really charismatic."

Adventure Club

"THE SEVEN-YEAR-OLD ADVENTURE CLUB," he called it, the words capitalized, of course. I was in second grade, living in the house by the river. I think he and my mother set up the name of the club so he wouldn't have to take in every kid in the neighborhood. The eight of us were enough of a handful on the hikes he led.

The abandoned quarry with the steep rock walls was only a mile from our house. That would be a nightmare in this era of lawsuits and liability; then, it was just a great adventure. We scrambled over sharp volcanic rock and through thickets of honeysuckle to get a chance to look over the edge into the pit. The metal monsters of quarry machines were far below and silent on a Saturday, but fascinating all the same. Some kids danced close to the edge of the rock, others hung back. My father led us all back home like a gaggle of assorted ducklings.

Did he take us all to the railroad yard, or was that a special walk I got to take only by myself with him, and later with both him and my son? He loved finding the secret places behind properties, brushy wildernesses in the neighborhood landscape, and emerging through some startled person's backyard with a comradely wave. Tagging along, I hung my head with shyness, embarrassment, pride.

There Once was a Puffin

> OH, THERE ONCE was a puffin,
> just the shape of a muffin
> and he lived on an island in the
> deep blue sea.
>
> He ate little fishes
> which were most delicious
> and he ate them for breakfast
> and he ate them for tea.

"The Puffin" was my favorite rhyme in the big poetry book with the cardboard covers, right along with "The Tale of Custard the Dragon" and "The Owl and the Pussycat." The poem was on a page by itself. The color picture showed a very cute bird with a big orange bill, on a small rock surrounded by blue, blue water, and he was crying big blue tears.

> But the poor little puffin
> he couldn't play nothing
> for he didn't have anyone
> to play with at all.

My mother read the poem to me over and over, in my tiny bedroom with the swan wallpaper, which she must have applied to the walls. It was supposed to be bathroom wallpaper, because it had swans and those were the rules of decorating, but it was my wish and my room at age five, so I got the swans to live with for several years. I imagine my mother loved this poem, too, with its lonely protagonist and the comfort of the rocking waves of rhymes.

> So he sat on his island
> and he cried for a while
> and he felt very lonely
> and he felt very small.

In the end, the puffin gives up eating fishes in order to be friends with them

> and the puffin eats pancakes
> like you and like me.

This ending may have comforted my mother as well as me, when finding companions sometimes seemed about as realistic as finding hot pancakes on an isolated island in the northern sea. She didn't have friends, no one to hang out or gossip with.

Eccentric

I GREW UP IN AN ECCENTRIC family, at least by the standards of the working-class neighborhood where we lived. We were not Catholic, not even religious, not Italian or Irish, and my father did not leave for work in the morning.

My friends were shocked that I never called my parents "Mom" and "Dad," and certainly not "Mommy" and "Daddy." From back before I can remember, they were "Myra" and "Jack." I guess that they decided this for political reasons, because they believed kids should be equal to grownups. My sister Kathy called them Myra and Jack until she hit kindergarten and learned quickly that it was weird to call your parents by their names, so she switched to Mom and Dad. Despite the teasing of my friends, I never changed the way I addressed them.

We had moved to this neighborhood when I was four, to the house by the salt river that led to the harbor. My father opened his own small electrical engineering business and finally got away from the bosses that drove him crazy. He detested working for other people. My mother later told me that before I was born, he would often arrive home so angry after working in a factory that he went to the basement and beat on a punching bag until he could come upstairs and be civil.

Jack was a terrible businessman, constantly underestimating how long jobs would take, so he never made much money. He also couldn't stand deadlines and would put things off until the very last minute, being covertly angry at himself for doing it, then get hair-trigger tense as the deadline approached. My mother tried to get him to start on projects early, but the more she pushed, the more he dug in his heels, and the more he procrastinated, the more she felt responsible for trying to get him going.

Jack's business occupied increasing portions of the house by the river, beginning at the bottom level. In it he employed my mother, who did the bookkeeping and secretarial duties and often did wiring and assembly work, too. Jack attracted eccentric, talented employees like Howard, the alcoholic, Rudy, the brilliant "cripple" who had polio, and Ray, the cartoonist.

Rudy Mertz

I REMEMBER RUDY swinging himself on his wooden crutches over the basement floor of Jack's shop. He said "Good morning" in that deep New York voice, then swung in arcs like an upside-down gibbon, over to the workbench where he placed the crutches on the floor, straightened up, and set to work. He pulled the schematics towards him, found the color-coded wires in the right lengths, and heated up the soldering iron. As the acrid scent of solder and rosin rose into the air, he settled in for a good meditative stretch of straightforward work. He fused the shiny solder blobs neatly onto the joinings: wire to resistor, resistor to capacitor, black wire to ground. Then he took up the cording to harness the wires together into little highways of electrical traffic, colorful braids of individual wires running together before they took off in other directions.

As Rudy continued his patient work, he would always stop to smile at me if I went near his bench. There was a humor behind his remarks that didn't always make sense to me, but I never felt he was laughing at me, rather at the crazy world we lived in.

Decades letter, a few years after Jack died, I asked my mother for Rudy's phone number and took him a computer that I was ready to give away. I visited him for a couple of long conversations. He told me that in those days, it had been extremely hard for anyone disabled to get a job.

"They tended to think your mind was crippled, too. Jack was the best employer I had. But you know, he laid me off, too, when times got hard. He laid me off before the others."

"Oh, I'm sorry to hear that."

"Yeah.... Then he hired me back six months later. Still, he gave me real work to do; he could see I had a mind. I had fun in his shop."

A Summer Day

IT WAS A TYPICAL JULY day in our house by the river when I was about eight—no school, nothing much to do. After breakfast I wandered down to the dock that Jack had built, where the tides of the estuary came and went. The tide was receding from the oyster-shell beach. I lay on my stomach on the warm wooden planks of the dock and watched the tiny fish dart among the reeds. Then I took a glass jar and captured some of the clear shrimp to watch them swim around and around, their myriad legs coordinated in waves. After a while the tide had gone out past the dock, it was just mud out there, and I got tired of watching the fiddler crabs, so I released the shrimp and walked back up the path to the back yard. I found my friend Rose Marie and some of the other kids and we organized into a game of cowboys and Indians, dying spectacularly on the sloped lawn of Rose Marie's house.

At noon I heard Myra calling. "I gotta go," I told the kids. We dispersed.

I climbed up the outside wooden steps to the back door of the kitchen, on the floor above my father's shop. The shop faced the sloping backyard so that it was at ground level in back, underground at the front of the house. My father and his "guys," the two employees, were working there. Myra sent me down to the corner store for some fresh Italian bread, fragrant in a white paper wrapper, and some liverwurst that Mr. Marco sliced from the roll and weighed out for me. Liverwurst on Italian bread with mayonnaise—heaven! Myra and Jack and I ate lunch at the Formica table in the kitchen.

After lunch Jack went back to work and I asked Myra to play a game of Parcheesi.

"Well, I have to go down to the shop and send out some bills," she said, "but that can wait a bit. Let's play."

And we did, fiercely and with laughter. I read for a while, some fairy tales from the library, my eight-year-old body draped over the wing chair, one leg swinging while I absorbed this imaginary world.

Then I walked through my front-room bedroom and down the inside stairs to the shop. I had told Jack I would sort some boxes of screws and bolts. He touched my shoulder and steered me towards the cluttered workbench where I perched on a tall steel stool.

"You see, they come in different sizes and different fineness of threads. You'll get good at telling the 6:32 from the 8:32—see how the 8:32 is just a bit thicker? Then those 4:40s are smaller and the threads are finer. Here are samples of all of them."

I think he paid me twenty-five cents an hour, which was fine with me.

I worked for maybe an hour or two, until my fingers smelled of oil and steel. I looked at the bin where I'd put the 6:32 screws and I found one or two mistakes. "I finished all the ones you gave me," I told Jack.

"Great work," he said. "You're very good at this, you have a good eye. Tomorrow I'll show you about soldering." I was pleased; soldering was what the grownups did.

At the Beach

I WAS ALWAYS EXCITED on the occasions when we went to the big sandy public beach on Long Island Sound. There were hordes of kids, beach blankets, concession stands, and real waves. At eight years old I'd been learning to swim in a summer program at the YWCA but I wasn't very confident. Myra and Jack were parked on towels and I went a short way down the beach to bob up and down in the waves.

A man about the age of my parents approached me and offered to help me swim.

"No thanks," I said.

"Aw, come on. I can see you need help." And he put his hands on me, clumsily trying to help. Then I felt his fingers inside the crotch of my bathing suit. I wiggled away. He came back and did it again. I squirmed away. I had no thought of yelling, "Stop it!" That would embarrass him. I felt it would be wrong to speak up. It would not help.

I ran back to my parents, who were still sitting on their towels.

"You OK?" Myra asked.

"Sure," I said.

No Stories

My family had no stories, or very few. Some parents tell a lot of stories about past or present relatives, their kids, or their own childhoods. My parents never told me how they met, for example. I think both Myra and Jack wanted desperately to get away from their birth families, for quite different reasons. And they believed that the way to make the hurt go away was to ignore it.

My mother never talked about her growing up. Sometimes I asked questions. "What was it like when you were in high school?"

"Oh, that was so long ago. There's no use going back there."

Much later, during the nine months when she knew she was dying, she was willing to tell me a bit more. "You'd better ask now," she said wryly, "because you won't get another chance."

It was then that she said, "One thing you can say for my mother—she kept the family together and held onto our house during the Depression."

"Wow, that must have been hard, your father dying and the Depression and three girls to raise."

"It was."

"How did she do it?"

"She took in sewing, and we had a boarder. I don't know, but she did it."

It was the only good thing I heard Myra say about her mother. Her father was ill with Lou Gehrig's disease all the time she was in high school; he finally died when she was about twenty-three. Her mother was a busy, tightly-wound woman from the little I remember. I don't know what was between them but I remember when I was college-age, Myra told me she didn't like her mother. She didn't say why. When her mother died in a nursing home in Maryland, Myra did not tell me she was gone until months later, and I don't know whether she attended a funeral.

From the way Myra dismissed my inquiries, I gathered that her past was too painful for her to consider. I heard the bare bones from her dynamic, talkative sister, Aunt Virginia, and tried to imagine the rest. Circumstances limited Myra's horizons—no college, few options for independence.

My father's distance from his family had different roots. Where Myra may have felt neglected in her family, Jack was the cherished only child. His family had money and roots in Southern aristocracy. Although love and position gave him a sense of privilege, he felt smothered and constrained by the Catholicism and propriety of his family, my mother told me.

Jack's form of rebellion was left-wing politics. He joined the Communist Party in the 1930s and had a collection of Communist literature that he locked away in a box stored in the eaves. Despite spending hours in the attic exploring family treasures, I didn't know that box existed until near the time he died. Jack secretly organized labor unions in the steel mills where he worked as an engineer in the late 1930s.

I imagine that the socialist movement also encouraged its members to attempt to disown their pasts, especially privileged pasts. As newlyweds in 1938, my parents were pleased to be swept up in the movement—that much they told me. Perhaps they were also glad to shed the oppressive bonds of their upbringing.

The Egg Man

THE KITCHEN WAS COLD and full of gray light. My mother stood at the gas stove facing the back door, where stairs led down to the yard and to the river. I was at the Formica table, gray marbleized surface and aluminum grooves wrapping around. A crack opened down the middle where the leaves could pop up, the crack always gummed with crumbs and butter. There was a window behind me and one across the room—with three sides exposed to the northwest wind, this kitchen was drafty in winter.

Old Mr. Barrett stumped up the flight of wooden stairs to the door, rapped on the door, and came in. His odor could have knocked me off my chair, the smell of hen manure and the intimate life of chickens. His house, with its coops, was three doors down the street, on the uphill side. He stood by the back door ill at ease, with his gray-whiskered old man face, denim overalls, and a striped cotton railroad cap. My father could talk to anyone, and usually did, perhaps more easily than to his family. They talked about the weather and who among the neighbors was sick or had a new dog.

"You can come to the front door, you know," my mother said. "It's a lot easier than climbing those steps."

"Naw, this is OK," Mr. Barrett said, left the two dozen eggs, and clumped down the stairs.

"Why do you ask him in?" I said after he left. "He smells awful."

"He's a person, too," my father said. "That's just his work, the chickens. Underneath the smell, he's just a person."

Speak Up

He stood over me in the basement bathroom. I was about six, and I had a wet undershirt in my hand that I had accidentally dropped into the clean toilet. The pull-chain toilet was in front of me, the massive clawfoot bathtub at my left.

Just yesterday, in the workroom of the shop, Jack had lectured me on the Fifth Amendment. It was McCarthy times. "You have the right to remain silent," he said, "you don't have to incriminate yourself. If some court or committee or policeman asks you questions, you are in America, you never have to tell anything that will show that you are guilty. This is the Constitution; it is the highest law of the land."

His lectures went along with the posters, but the posters were way back in the cellar part of his basement shop. The men who worked for him were in the forward rooms, the rooms with a bit of daylight. Rudy, the gentle man who had polio, struggled down the steep stone steps summer or winter with his wooden crutches. Ray, the comic, ambled into the office or the assembly room and made wisecracks. The tiger cat strolled in from the marigold garden, past my father's heaped-up desk and my mother's tidier one. In the back room were the parts cabinets, cigar boxes of switches, tubes, and connectors, spools of solder, racks of tools for assembling big mysterious electrical machines that lit up or whirred.

Down in the furnace room, a poster with a picture of a large-eyed child said plaintively, "I am TOO an American," in the immigrant child's voice. "I love living here. Don't call me a spic or a wop or a foreigner. I belong here too." And there was a poster of the leader of the Amistad slave ship uprising, fifty years before Steven Spielberg discovered the story.

"You have to tell me," he said towering over me in the bathroom. "How did it get wet? What did you do?" Silence filled my mouth. Shadow was in my backbone, water in my knees, stubborn fear in my chin. If I were the poster child, would he hear me? What happened to the man who could teach patiently? "Speak up," he thundered.

What kind of voice could come out of me? "Speak up!" *But you said, just yesterday...but you said...*

Family Vacation

GOING ON VACATION with my father was a roller coaster, beginning with his inability to get started. My mother packed it all: the clothes, the towels, the lunches. He always needed one more thing: the canteen, the shovel, the tools. Finally, they locked the big front door and we took off for the Catskills, on the way to visit my sister Suzie at her school for the retarded. The first miles were pretty safe, because he had seen all the sights before. By the time we got into New York State, it would get chancier.

"There's an octagonal house!" he said. My mother sighed in the front seat, knowing what was coming next.

"Let's stop and talk to the people living there."

"Do you have to? We do want to get to the cabin before dinner."

"Don't you want to come?"

"No."

"I'll just be a minute."

She slumped down and rolled her eyes, and my shoulders tightened—which one to be loyal to?

He knocked on the door. Watching from the car, I could see him gesturing to the man who opened the door. They talked; they walked around the outside of the house; they disappeared through the door. Twenty minutes later, he emerged to tell us the details of how they fit the rooms into an octagonal house, when it was built, and how long the people had been living there.

Boo-boos

MY FRIEND COLLEEN'S HOUSE could not have been more different from mine. The tiny, dark living room was strewn with toys. Her brothers tussled on and off the couch, yelling. In the middle of the chaos, her mother was ironing at a board, clothes basket by her feet, radio blaring nearby. Colleen's father was at work, of course.

We raced in from the backyard where Colleen had just fallen and scraped her knee. "Mommy!" she wailed. "I got a boo-boo."

"Let me see," her mother said, setting down the iron and coming over to the chair where Colleen had plunked herself down. It was a slight scrape not requiring a bandage.

"Will you kiss it better?"

"Of course," her mother said, kissing the grubby knee and then hugging Colleen.

"Better now?"

"Yes."

I felt I was witnessing an exotic ritual. Kissing it better? Casual hugs? My family was made of sterner stuff and I didn't expect any such nonsense when I was hurt.

The Spartan Boy

MY FATHER WAS FASCINATED by the stories about ancient Greece he had learned as a boy in private schools.

"Now, the Athenians and the Spartans were always fighting," he said to me one afternoon when I was in grade school. We were in the back yard where he had been raking leaves. "And the Athenians had a lot of freedoms, but the Spartans were well-disciplined."

I must have looked blank.

"The Spartans believed in plain living and hard training. They brought up young boys to play in the cold with no warm clothes, to eat very little, and to sleep on cold marble beds."

"Why?"

"So they would be very good soldiers; they were tough and obedient."

I wasn't sure if he was admiring that or not.

"One of the stories they told was of a boy who stole a fox and hid it beneath his toga next to his skin."

I could picture that. But I didn't know why he took the fox.

"The fox bit him beneath the toga, gnawing at his 'vitals'."

What are those? I thought. Jack pointed to the area below his ribs. That would hurt a lot and you could die.

"But the boy was so brave that he did not tell anyone that he had the fox. In fact he bled to death rather than tell."

My father told me the story of that Spartan boy when I was six or seven years old. Around that time I began to have nightmares in which I was frozen to the ground while out of the sunset over the river, a fox grew closer and larger.

Going Upriver

ABOUT ONCE EACH SUMMER as I was growing up, the family would make an expedition up the river in the wooden boat. Myra generally made a fuss about taking the time and trouble, but once we were launched, she had a good time.

Someone had to plan it carefully to account for weather and tides. We needed to go upstream on a rising tide, but not too high yet, because we had to slip under wooden train trestles that were close to the water. Myra would pack the lunches and water. Jack would carry the motor down to the boat and ask me to bring the oars along. He got the gas-oil mixture and the spare cotter pin for when the propeller struck something. And the bailing can—essential equipment.

We all went down to the dock and brought in Old Ironsides, the boat, on its running line, stepping down the ladder and into the bottom. Jack wound the cotton clothesline around the starting pulley, then yanked. A few oily grumbles came from the motor. Then he pulled again, and it started. In twenty seconds or so, he adjusted the throttle, while I unclipped the rope from the line, and we went off. Past the red stone pier next door, covered with seaweed and barnacles, past the reeds and the salt marsh, under a bridge where the river narrowed to a real flowing stream.

The roar of the motor made conversation difficult. Jack let me take the tiller and steer the boat until we came to the next bridge. This was the low railroad bridge, and he took the steering back again while we ducked down low and smelled the creosote, hoping nothing would drop off the massive trestles into our hair in the dark. Back out again, we had a clear run of river for several miles where we never saw another human being.

Great blue herons took off laboriously as we approached, and once Myra pointed in great excitement. What was she pointing at? Seemed like nothing there. Jack slowed the boat to a crawl. "Oh, I see it now," I breathed. A bittern, brown and white stripes, beak pointed up in perfect camouflage.

As we inched our way upstream past the willow trees and floating logs, the river grew shallower; we had to catch the upward tide to go very far at all. Inevitably, we struck a log or sandbar and the propeller disconnected. Inevitably, Jack swore at it. But most of the day was an enchanted, sunburnt ride through a private wilderness full of turtles, fish, and birds.

Sandals

In the summer Jack wore sandals. They had brown leather straps up the middle, other straps opening off like ribs, and dark gray rubber soles. He wore baggy shorts, white canvas, that flapped his thighs as he carried the oars down the narrow path in our back yard, to the river.

One day Jimmy Callahan, the eldest of the brood of trouble-making kids next door, stopped my father with the question, "Whatcha doin' wit' your mommy's shoes on?" For twenty years after we moved away, Jack told that encounter with delight.

His pleasure in the story? Was it the child's ignorance that a man could wear sandals? The confusion of mommy and wife? The joy of being unconventional, that was certainly part of his enjoyment. He repeated the question every time in the same tone of childish suspicion, "Whatcha doin' wit' your mommy's shoes on?"

≈ 4 The Dance

ON A SEPTEMBER EVENING, I entered a studio to start my new "Authentic Movement" class with Rita, who had been one of my movement teachers for six years and was also a friend. We met in a large, airy room, full of evening light. Plain white walls framed big windows overlooking farm land and parking lots. Eight or nine people were gathered, mostly women, several of whom I knew. I felt comfortable in this setting, a place where emotional, creative, and spiritual threads could weave together. I expected the people there would be interested in inner development.

After brief introductions, Rita re-oriented us to the form: "The idea is to notice your inner impulses, and simply move or be still in response to those impulses. Keeping your eyes closed is a way to bring your attention inward, away from the appearance of the movement and towards noticing your own desires. In this first moving time, everyone will move, with me as witness. After that, you all will have a chance to talk about your own movement, and I will respond briefly, if you wish. Later in the year you will begin to witness one another and to respond, but we'll take our time with that."

Rita then went on to remind us of the safety rules: open your eyes if you are doing large movements; if you come in contact with another mover, each has the choice to follow his or her own impulses to remain in contact or move away; do no harm to yourself, to others, or to the room; all material that is witnessed is confidential, not to be talked about outside of the group. We agreed that movers could make sounds as part of their moving; this was a negotiable issue.

Once I started moving, it was clear that all my new material was at the fore.

Knock-kneed, holding my hand in front of That Place, I move in a shuffling walk around the room. I feel so naked; it is good that just Rita is watching, this time. Just keep doing this same movement, I'm not ready to move on. I feel ashamed and young.

Fortunately, the Authentic Movement format does not require any kind of disclosure. After we all moved, with Rita watching, we each had a chance to speak. I don't remember what I said, but I do know that I didn't even hint at my abuse issues in this group setting until many months later.

At another early meeting, a man named Warren, who was thin and tense with a weedy-looking beard, said that he was dealing with childhood abuse issues.

He is braver or in a different place than I. I appreciate his opening that door, and my body goes through it.

Thighs glued together I walk, wiggle sideways, slide. I cannot imagine opening my thighs. I twist from side to side, my thighs so aware of one another. This is erotic? No, yes, no, yes. Pain in my belly. I am working here, privately. No words.

Around me I could hear footsteps of someone walking, a brushing sound as if someone was sweeping her hands over the wall, faint sighs and breaths.

In the sharing time afterwards, I did not have a lot I wanted to say to the group, just noting that it was a new space and new issues. Rita was acting as the witness and responder for us all.

"What do you see that is new?" I asked her. She had seen me in movement for several years.

"There's something different in the lower half of your body, something that seems important." she said. "My image is of you being quite young."

I heard her response gratefully. She did not need to know my issues, but could respond to movements she saw, without interpretation. I felt witnessed and acknowledged. There was something vitally important to me about being able to be in that group setting and express what was happening to me non-verbally, without anyone having to know explicitly about it, and without having to put it into words.

As this movement group met week after week, we gradually learned to create a safe and sacred circle where many feelings and images could come through our bodies. There were simple rituals that helped to create safety. We sat in a circle at the start of each moving session, when Rita told us the structure for the evening. Then we stood in a circle and moved backward until we encompassed the whole space. Rita rang a bell, and the movement began. At the end of the movement time, she again rang a bell and gave a few minutes for completion and re-entry into a more conscious state. At first, Rita was the sole witness.

Authentic Movement work invites the unconscious to come. Movement can arise spontaneously and later be integrated consciously by the mover. As I moved, I sometimes saw colors or heard voices, along with the sensations from the movement. One voice kept coming that fall.

> *"After all," the voice says, the definitive male voice, "after all it's not like she was raped. It's not like she was old enough to remember. It's not like she really was hurt. It's not like in some families."*

I did not know how to place these fragments and I certainly was not ready to speak of them in the movement group. I brought them to Sarah in therapy, where she took them seriously. I loved that she welcomed the material that came up in my movement group and in my private writing. I could imagine a therapist wanting all the work to come under her watchful eye, but Sarah was the opposite. Not only did she validate things that emerged in different ways and different places, but I sensed that she encouraged them so that the work would be my own and so that I would develop as many resources as possible.

In the moving, along with my pain and uncertainty, I often had moments of pure joy. Simple observation and appreciation of my body sensations gave me enormous highs. One of the great things about the movement practice was that it was not therapy, even though it brought up a lot of feelings that I could use in therapy. I did not feel I needed to be "on task," and so feelings could flow through—joyous one minute, frightening the next. I had many times of moving with sheer delight in my body.

> *Happy today sometimes. Warming up in bubbles and slides and prances. A sensual moving, following sensation, no goal. Against the wall, my body feels the pressure of the surface as support and enjoyment, inhabiting the relationship with the wonderful, neutral being that lives in this "wall." My skin loves sliding on the floor, circling and searching with my hands, following a circuitous path.*

EACH WEEK I SEEMED to be dealing with the abuse issues in one way or another. Sometimes it was through group dynamics.

> *Today some of the women wanted it to be quiet in the room, so I said OK along with the others and we agreed to have a silent moving time, no sounds at all. I could see how silence is useful. But then I hated it so much. Silenced by women again! Be good. Shut up. Don't tell. For my mother's sake I was supposed to shut up? Myra was helpless/needy/fragile like these women here who so insistently say they need silence. Like Pandora not supposed to open the box, not open her mouth. They did it! They put all that stuff there. It's not my fault, not my fault, no no no no no no no!*
>
> *Expecting to be silenced, to be backed into a corner by women who act helpless and hurt so I have to shut up and shrink small.*

I watched my own reactions curiously, looking for hints. In my relations with Myra at that time, she clearly did not want to talk about anything real or painful. I felt I had to be quiet and not tell anything painful because she was too fragile.

During the sharing time, I said how hard the silence was for me and how I worked with it by making fists and silently screaming. It was a huge relief to allow the feelings to emerge and to speak of them—so different from "normal" human interactions where I felt I wasn't supposed to have such irrational reactions.

Another week, we were again asked to be silent. Again, I had to work with my strong feelings about being silenced.

> *We are told not to speak. I am huddled and feeling very sorry for this small person who has to hold it, hold it all and not speak, not speak, not speak.*
>
> *Maybe, maybe I can show it someday but not speak. Maybe moving is a way to speak without fear of being attacked, fear of being accused of being wrong, very wrong and bad.*

Here, again, I did not have a clear memory or film-clip of my mother silencing me. What I had were very strong feelings that I had to hide things, both for her sake and also so that I would not be made to feel wrong and bad.

Early in the year's cycle, this movement group had an all-day workshop where I paired with Warren, the man who was open about his working on issues of childhood abuse. At this workshop we had an opportunity to work intensively in pairs, witnessing one another and practicing the skill of giving non-judgmental, non-interpretive feedback.

Warren's movement was often disturbing for me to watch while I also felt an affinity with him and permission to go to dark places because of his presence. His movement work was passionate and often hinted at violence. Sometimes he cowered in the corner with his hands over his head. Other times he flung his arms forward as if hitting an invisible person, or flailed around the room. I was drawn to the explicitness of his feelings. I think most of us in there were shy of him, and I was the only one who volunteered to work with him at the all-day workshop.

I would never have said it aloud, but Warren scared me. I think he was a Viet Nam vet, and he surely was on some kind of disability pension; he did not go to work like most of us, and he mentioned being in some kind of recovery group.

Is this what it means to be recovering from abuse? That you can't hold a job, you're outside the mainstream? I feared that this might be my path, that I would really fall apart, and that I would be seen as disabled and marginalized. I had no other models, so I didn't know what recovery might look like. I was afraid also because I felt so explosive inside, like I would shatter into pieces or explode in rage or dissolve totally in tears—my feelings were so huge that I could not see how I would function if I really allowed them to emerge. Sarah told me later that feelings are enormous to a child, especially when they have not been allowed to be expressed. I felt I couldn't be acting like a grownup while having my strong feelings. Perhaps the idea of disability was attractive, too, a part of me wanting to stop trying to act normal and just fall apart.

That day in the workshop was intense, both my own movement and my witnessing of Warren's.

> *So aware of what he said about dealing with abuse. Moving, I go to an expanse of space with this young girl in it, a space of doubt and wonder. I ask what is it? Will I ever know what it means to have these legs locked together? Will I ever become clearer than this muddy painful in-between place? Meanwhile, I walk awkwardly with my thighs locked together, wondering how this will be seen.*
>
> *This child learned so early how to cope and conform and be good and survive—I honor that. And now so much later I learn how to be tender with her needs. I fold into the corner of the wall. I honor the sudden tiredness, the weepiness at the corner of my eye, the sense of burden and pain.*

After the movement I sat with Warren on the floor near a window, with other pairs of dancers murmuring in other corners of the room. I told him, "I'm dealing with early issues of abuse, too. That's what my movement was about today." I did not get specific or spill my guts. The delicate dance of needing to be seen and recognized but also needing to protect myself goes on right into the present day. People's reactions vary widely and can be painful to receive. I ended that day of workshop excited at having worked intensely with a partner who shared some issues.

> *But I need to acknowledge that the dance workshop raised a lot of pain, anger, and other feelings for me. It is not all positive and lovely. I believe in the power of healing and the ability of the self to open, to feel hurt and ultimately to heal. Meanwhile, there is pain.*

At the end of that day, I spoke with Rita and she talked about my watching Warren, which she had noted as powerful and connected. I mentioned to Rita that there were issues coming up for me. I hoped she'd take me up on this and connect it to Warren's issues on abuse. She passed it by.

I began to realize that I needed Rita to know what I was going through so she could help me contain my feelings. A few days later, I took my heart in my hand and called to tell her what I was working on. She said she could see from my movement that I was working on something deep and important and early, even though she had not known what it was.

"Do you want to say more about what happened?"

"No, not really. It was early, it was sexual. It was my father, I'm pretty sure."

"Oh my."

"Part of me is clear it really happened, but part of me is still saying 'No way.'"

"I can imagine that. It's big."

"It's important to have some people know, but I have to be pretty careful who I tell."

"I am glad you told me. It's fine to bring that material to the group as you have been doing. Are you working with it in therapy?"

"For sure."

"Oh, I'm glad you have that support. You know, you have such a way of working deeply. It is beautiful and clear to witness. I am really happy to have you in the group."

Those were just the words I needed to feel cared for. She not only supported me, she delighted in me. I told her I loved her. Feeling enormous gratitude, I wrote,

> *I am so thankful. This work can lead to a deeper love. Now that she knows, she will see more and differently. I trust her to see me in those places.*

AS THE GROUP WENT ON meeting weekly through the year, we did more witnessing of one another, and that is when I felt I should disclose my issues. I felt I was being less than candid. In the thick of the memories, it was hard to know how to protect myself. Finally, I did tell the whole group that I was working on childhood sexual abuse. I remember all eight of us sitting cross-legged on the floor near one of the windows. As I looked around the circle after I spoke, I saw solemn looks and felt respect, a quiet holding.

Because of the format, there was no verbal response. Amazingly, the building did not cave in and people did not flee.

A few weeks later, I was again paired with Warren.

Warren told me yesterday that he sees my work as brave and revealing. Yes. What that touches, makes me cry. I need to be seen. I need to have my struggle seen compassionately. I need to open this up, yet be protected.

At the end of the year, the group had a special session to integrate the work and begin to say goodbye. We all had time to move in the circle and be witnessed.

Happy again. My feet on the floor such a joy! So many sensations I can't follow but I can follow, oh my the pressure, the toe joints, ankles wagging, arms alive with weight. I could be here forever.

And it becomes a prowl, an animal prowl, claws up and striking, snarls arising playfully. A duet of sound with another mover, matching animal sounds, until I want to move on.

I turn my knees in and allow a bit of the question, the problem for the little girl, the vulnerable possibility of her abuse and misuse, to be there. I walk with that, painfully but keeping it at a bit of a distance.

Then hands raise to ward off—no! No! Quickly I ask myself, what do I need to do?

My left hand is crumpled by my face, needy like a child. My right hand shields and comforts the left and I turn slowly, soothing myself into no-pain. When I stop turning, my head goes back to cry, my mouth opens to yell silently, my breath comes. I feel my chest, the pain or joy cracking it open. Heart.

My breath comes, that sound that is human: here I am, I am mortal, I can feel pain, here is my offering to you.

Then we were invited to show several minutes of movement to the whole group. I chose to follow out the last part of that sequence for the group: the crumpled hand, the cradling, the opening chest. Different people saw different things in my movement, with one woman noting the joy in part of it.

Warren said he saw me being at risk and exposed. Afterwards, as we were leaving, I thanked him for seeing and saying that. He said, "I see a lot of vulnerability in your mouth. It can be upsetting to watch. Sometimes I've been disturbed by your movement. If you get odd responses it could be that people are unable to hold and live with the vulnerability they see."

"Oh, that's helpful—difficult but helpful. Thanks. I really have enjoyed working with you."

I was sad to end that group with whom I had shared so much, but I knew I would keep on doing Authentic Movement. And I have. Moving and witnessing in groups give me opportunities to keep experiencing growth as struggle and joy. The process continues to stir up unconscious material. The loosely-knit Authentic Movement community provides a large group for support. It takes my inner work beyond therapy, making a bridge to the larger world.

≈ 5 Relations

AFTER A TWO-HOUR DRIVE, I arrived at my mother's house around noon on the day before Thanksgiving, three months after Revelation Day. She lived in the same modest two-story house in a solid working-class suburb where she and my father, then she alone, had lived for the last twenty-five years. The yard had been raked by her yard man, but was showing some signs of neglect in the untrimmed bushes; I would have to get to those in spring.

As I walked up the concrete steps, I felt a familiar blend of affection and burden descend on me. Although I had been to visit her twice since the revelation and talked on the phone every Sunday morning, I had not mentioned my returning memory to her. If I even thought about bringing it up, fear choked me, and I knew I would need to be a lot further on in the process before I could say anything to her. I had heard, and could well believe, that family members often deny that anything could possibly have happened in their family, and I was not ready to risk either the rift that might develop or the threat to my own fragile belief in myself.

My mother was the arbiter of reality in the family. My father had been impractical, enthusiastic, idealistic. Because Jack dashed off in all directions, Myra was the voice of reason. He became more extreme in his lack of responsibility because he knew she would pick up the pieces, while she was angry at him and acted hyper-responsible because of his lack. Because she was the stable center, it was hard to think of negotiating a new truth with her.

Myra greeted me at the door and smiled at me. She really did love me, I knew that, so I smiled back as I edged past her with armloads of groceries. As soon as I finished carrying in the extras that I had brought, she offered me something to eat and then started her lists of things to do: the meals to prepare, the shopping, the things to fix in the house. "I don't know what to do about snacks for Will; I got chips and salsa and bread and three kinds of cheese and there's ice cream and soda, but I don't know if it's enough."

At that point she was 82 years old, living alone, and did not drive. She hired someone to do the shopping for her and seldom went out of the house. Her sole friend was another elderly woman who lived across the street. Myra would see her coming and groan, because Arlie usually perched on the sofa, emitting a powerful smell of dogs, and delivered a long monologue of complaint with my mother listening politely.

Myra could often be found lying on the sofa reading a murder mystery. Otherwise she kept busy with housework and crafts such as weaving, beadwork, and needlework, which she planned fanatically and enjoyed intensely. She made all her own dresses, since she hated shopping and could not find what she liked. She had dozens of polyester knit dresses made from just two patterns—long-sleeved and sleeveless—in print after print. For years, she made many of my clothes and my sister Kathy's, too. Her sewing was legendary; every seam was perfect, every garment adjusted to fit just right. She hated shoddy work. I felt both admiration and irritation at the way she had found her own way of doing things and stuck to it.

The day I arrived, I kept busy as usual, putting in the storm doors, fixing the shower head, moving a little table near her sewing machine, and so forth. I had taken on the chores my father used to do before he was disabled by the Parkinson's.

"Would you take a look at that spot on the bedroom ceiling? I can't see it very well."

"What about it? It's been there a while, right?"

"Well, I can't tell if it has gotten any larger. The roof man said he fixed the leak, but I'm worried about it."

"Why don't you ask him to come look?"

"Oh, I couldn't do *that*."

"Why not? That's his job."

"Oh, I don't want to bother him."

For reasons that got clearer and clearer, her lack of assertion irked me deeply.

ON THANKSGIVING DAY Myra and Kathy and I were in the kitchen cooking the turkey and stuffing, mashed potatoes, and pumpkin pie. Kathy's husband and stepdaughter and my son were settled in the living room beyond arms' reach. Myra was basting the turkey when she said, "What shall we have for a vegetable—peas or beans?"

"I've never liked peas much. Let's have beans," I said.

"French cut or regular cut?"

"Let's do the French cut."

"Shall we have almonds with them?"

"Sure. I'll toast them."

"Should we have sour cream with the beans?"

Can't she decide anything? Or just leave it to me? "No, let's not."

"Oh, but I got some just for this."

She wants the sour cream. Why didn't she say so? "Fine." There was a picador quality to her indecisiveness, a need to engage me in her worries.

Finally the six of us sat down to eat. We kept to the safe topics with news of family, comments on the food. I was still screaming inside, but I had no idea what to do about it. I wasn't about to blurt out, "Jack abused me when I was three." I couldn't see how to find a greater closeness with my mother or my sister. I wanted to talk about feelings and history, while they stayed with the ordinary.

It was another seemingly neutral day in the family. Nothing was said, no emotions surfaced. No conflict, no contact, no friction, no heat, no light. I felt complicitous, careful like the rest of them.

My mother was skilled at distancing. As a child I didn't even think of running to her for hugs. These days, my only contacts with her were the brief ritual hugs of hello and goodbye. I saw her physical remoteness clearly when my son Will was young. Myra did not delight in squeezing that tender baby flesh; she did not hold him. My father, however, did like contact with him, and I have a lovely photograph of him holding Will at age three months, my father looking joyous and contented, proud. I think my father was the one to hold me when I was quite small, so when he violated that trust, he sent me off into a lost, lost land.

My difficult feelings about my mother were of long standing, but my new revelations made them all the more urgent. That night I went upstairs to my bedroom early to try to make sense of the intense feelings invoked by the quiet family scenes. Sitting in the wooden rocking chair, I felt a tearing pain in my chest.

"Little Jane, what is it?" I asked softly.

At first there was just a confusion of upset feelings. Then a childish voice said, "Everybody is so careful. I hate being careful. I want to be carefree or careless or caring but not careful. I want to be loving and warm, I want to be angry, I want to get through the walls. I want lumpy and colorful and wet and messy and squishy and noisy and red and yellow and smelly and tasty and all kinds of alive."

"Oh, you sound lonely."

"I am! How come I feel so wrong? How come no one says anything real in my family? Am I asking too much?"

"Little one, you have a great capacity for directness and intimacy. You didn't make the family this way. You deserve love, caring, warmth, honesty. It's OK to be know that you deserve better, even if you don't get it."

"But who will take care of me?" the young voice wailed.

"Please let me hold you. I want to be the grownup you never had, the one who really listens to the things you have words for and don't have words for. I want you to be exactly who you are. You don't have to be a convenient, considerate, cheerful child the way you were for Myra." I rocked and hugged myself until the sobs diminished.

THE DAY AFTER THANKSGIVING, I drove out to pick up my sister Suzie at her foster home while Kathy and Myra prepared the traditional lunch of turkey leftovers, toast, carrot and celery sticks, warmed-over stuffing, and pumpkin pie. We always saw Suzie on the day after the holiday.

I invited Will to ride with me, hoping he'd be willing to talk. At twenty-one, he was a tall, serious young man, a college student on the West Coast. I'd always felt close to him, but he was moody. At times, we talked of feelings and life issues with a depth that amazed me. Other times he was as silent as mud. Today he seemed sullen, although he'd readily agreed to come along for the ride. After getting monosyllabic answers to my questions about school and his social life, I gave up and talked to him about my work and friends. The new questions about my early life were too raw to share with him.

At her foster home, Suzie was ready and waiting, with an eager, shy smile. She was a little overweight and her bright-colored shirt billowed as she shuffled and puffed towards me. Her hair had less gray than mine, I noticed, and she was a little bald on top, which I could see because she was even shorter than I. I hugged her, saying, "My sister!"

"My sister," Suzie chuckled with pleasure.

"Happy Thanksgiving, Suzie." "Happy Thanksgiving, Jane."

"I'm glad to see you." "I'm glad to see you, too."

"How are you?" "I'm fine."

She preferred the ritual kinds of talk where the answers were clear. We went outside and I helped her into the car.

"How is work?"

"It's fine."

I filled her in on who would be there when she got there, but conversation beyond that point was hard to keep up. We stopped on the way to get some flowers for Myra. Suzie headed eagerly towards the brightest red and orange chrysanthemums, saying, "Get these ones!" Perhaps she enjoyed shopping so much because her early years were spent in a sheltered environment away from the bustle of stores.

Back at Myra's house, we sat down to lunch immediately, and Suzie was busy eating, politely asking for seconds. Her voice was hard to understand and she was not talkative, while my mother was also getting deaf. Communication was not easy. But Suzie was clearly glad to be there. My mother gave her a simple needlework kit, one of dozens that Suzie happily stitched over the years. After we sat a bit and tried to talk, I took Suzie and Will to the movies. I asked Myra if she wanted to go, but we all knew that the question was perfunctory since she rarely left the house.

The next morning my son slept till noon. After we had breakfast, Myra and I hung out in the kitchen making conversation.

"When do you suppose Kathy is coming?" she asked.

"I don't know. She said ten or eleven."

"Well, it's nearly eleven now," she said with an impatient gesture.

"Well, you know Kathy."

"Why don't you call her?"

"Let's wait a bit." I knew Kathy hated to be pushed. I poured another cup of coffee.

Myra made more jittery movements while I ignored them. "Really!" she said. "Why isn't she here?"

I went to the phone in the next room. "I'm just getting up!" she said shortly. "Did you have to call?"

"Sorry. It's just that Myra wanted to know."

Time went on while we waited. Kathy finally called to say she was too busy to come.

Myra fumed with disappointment, saying, "I never know what she is going to do. Thank heavens I can count on you!" I squirmed inside, uneasy about getting appreciation framed in that way. It had been a long time since Kathy's wild teenage years, but our roles as good girl and bad girl were always getting reinforced. At the same time, I had enough sense of duty, or perhaps it was love, to want to keep being dependable for Myra.

Not only was I the good girl of the family, I was supposed to be smart enough for two, since I was born as the substitute child for Suzie. A few years previously, my Aunt Virginia had given me the letters Myra wrote to her right after Suzie's diagnosis, saying that the doctors were urging them to have another child quickly and place Suzie in an institution. I was born less than a year and a half after she was, so I have to think they listened to the doctors. I earned perfect grades in school, played the piano, was quiet and obedient and shy. When there was tension between Myra and Jack, as there often was at the dinner table—he slamming objects around and huffing but not talking, she glaring back with locked jaw—I talked about school and tried to draw attention to defuse the tension.

SARAH LEANED FORWARD to listen as I described the weekend. "Myra always wants to keep busy. She hardly ever will sit and talk. When she does, it seems loaded with anxiety and misdirection."

"What do you mean by misdirection?"

"She says so urgently, 'What are we going to do about Congress? We have to do something.' And I know she's not going to write letters or even vote! It's like she wants me to solve the problem. I feel pushed and drawn into her anxiety. It doesn't feel like she's talking about what she's really worried about. And she's always so irritated about Kathy's behavior, it makes a cloud in the air."

Sarah said slowly, "You know, uproar can be a strategy for dealing with anxiety about something hidden. In some families it's a way of not revealing a secret, finding something extraneous to worry about and make noise about, a smokescreen."

"Oh, that makes sense." I paused to picture it. "Yes. Kathy and Myra are really good at playing uproar, like they have it choreographed. Kathy makes uncertainty, Myra reacts, then she calls on me to intervene. It's like a battlefield. How can I be there without being used to fix it all?"

I KNEW VERY LITTLE about Myra's childhood because she refused to talk about it, always saying, "That was so long ago." Or "I don't think about the past." Her two stories from her childhood both concerned illness. She had a shriveled toe, the fourth one on the left foot. It was hooked and missing the bone. She was two years old when she got gangrene in this toe. She almost did not live, but the doctor stayed all night, she said, all night till the fever broke. He said if she survived this, she would live to be a very old woman. In the other story she was about eleven years old and had severe pneumonia, in the days before antibiotics. Again they were not sure she would live, and she had to miss school nearly the whole of winter.

I wondered why these were the only two stories she would tell. My Aunt Virginia, my mother's sister, would talk, and talk, and talk. A few years earlier I had traveled to Maryland to interview Virginia about family history. Speaking into my tape recorder, she told me lots more than I wanted to know about long-dead great-uncles and great-aunts. Her responses to questions about my parents were sparser. Off-microphone, she sighed and said, "Myra sure was loyal, she was loyal to a fault." It was one of those hints that I knew I couldn't ask about. My guess is that she was referring to my father's several long, intense affairs with other women and my mother's staying with him, angrily, through it all.

Closed heart

There it is, hard kernel at the core
toughness I admired and hated.
What does it mean to love
somebody with a closed heart?

When asked about her past
she body-slammed
quick change of subject
There's no use talking about that
What are we going to have for dinner?

Towards the end my beggary worked
she gave crusts of answers.
Now her ashes sit
in a box at the funeral home

while I watch circles of raindrops
on wood, percussion on maple leaves,
every variety of water
on pine needle, shingle, metal.

What is love from a closed heart?
A thin thread pulled out between the hinges
an anxious querulous sound.

I never doubted that my mother loved me, that wasn't the issue. The content and quality of that love, however, were continual questions.

Trying to get through to Myra on a more emotional level. I attempted to share with her the ups and downs of my life. When I started to tell her about complications in my work life, she immediately tried to cheer me up or else changed the subject.

I tried showing my appreciation for what she had given me. One Saturday morning while I was visiting, we were in the kitchen with the sunlight coming through the window over the sink. She was talking about what she wanted me to do that day and beginning to repeat herself. I steeled myself to cut into her superficial talk and say, "You know, I keep remembering how you taught me so much of what I know about writing and about using English well. I use those skills all the time when I write grants or correct student papers."

"No, it was Jack who was so fascinated with words."

"Well, what I remember was you," I said.

"Schools these days don't teach anything. Kids just watch TV and don't have any attention span. They don't learn anything about language."

"But what I'm trying to say is I really value the way you taught me the precision of language and the use of words. I hope I've passed those on to Will. He seems to have a love of language, and it comes from you."

"Parents just don't get involved any more. You're an exception and Will is a wonderful kid. I don't know what the world is coming to these days."

It was frustrating that she couldn't seem to hear my appreciation. She adroitly flipped the conversation into the negative and away from the love I tried to offer. Inside me, Little Jane felt frantic.

What's wrong? I feel terrible but not much happened. Am I crazy? Why can't I get through to her? What am I doing wrong?

WHAT KIND OF FAMILY makes abuse possible? I wondered more and more about Myra's role, knowing she was not abusive herself, but becoming furious at her passivity and helplessness. It felt as if her silence and passivity fed Jack's pathology perfectly, allowing him to be irresponsible.

It might seem odd, but my energy was focused on Myra. My father remained a shadowy presence that year, the invisible one. I was beginning to be furious at my mother for not protecting me but I couldn't focus my rage on Jack. Of course, my mother was also physically present, while my father had been dead for a year and mentally gone for longer than that.

I began to see that there was something quite stable about the family structure, that both my mother and father contributed to a configuration that enabled him to abuse me and have it stay silent. In the society as a whole in the 1940s and 1950s, abuse was not discussed, neither physical nor sexual abuse. If my mother had spoken out, she would have risked her marriage and thus her financial base. I suspect there were many times when she wondered about leaving him, but she felt stuck.

A stable triangle: Myra's loyalty protects Jack's privilege, he gets what he wants. Jack's power keeps Myra silent. Jane's unquestioning child-love nourishes whatever love is there. And it is there.

≈ 6 Snippets

SARAH SAT BESIDE ME on her tweed couch in the warm oasis of her office. One by one, I handed her black-and-white photographs from the small stack I had brought to our session. "These are most of the photos I have from that house at Shell Beach when I was three and four, the place where I have the bathroom memory. Here's an early one where I'm on the beach in a winter coat, flinging sand."

"Oh! Your arms are wide open and your mouth wide open, too."

"Yes, I look intensely happy there. That was one of my father's favorite pictures.... Here's one where I'm playing in the yard with someone, must be the neighbor boy."

"You look strong and lively."

"But here's the one that gets me. It's kind of blurry because I had it enlarged."

There I was in overalls I'd outgrown, cotton socks and little leather shoes, hair pulled into stubby braids. A large wood-shingled house towered over me. I was holding the hand of a woman of perhaps fifty who was wearing a hat. "That was Mrs. Southwick, our landlady. Myra told me she liked her."

"You don't look happy at all," Sarah said.

"No. I look like a refugee. Smudges for eyes. I'm so little."

"You look drawn into yourself—quite the opposite of that beach picture."

"I feel so sorry for this little girl. I can believe she was abused." I sighed, then felt a rising tension. "But I don't remember any of the details. I don't have any pictures of what happened. How do I know if it's real? Do you believe me?"

"Yes, I believe you." she said, looking into my eyes. "A lot of people don't have clear memories, but there are signs."

"But I don't know whether to believe myself! It's so hard, this doubting."

"It *is*. That is one of the really painful parts of the work. But you can come back to it over and over, and ask me over and over."

I felt an enormous relief, a letting-go in my stomach. *I don't have to be all better right now. I can ask her again and again!*

"Think how many years it took while you had to deny it and pretend everything was OK. It took all that time for you to learn the patterns of denial. It will take time for the little girl to know that you believe her and that things are different now."

"But why can't I remember how it happened?" I wailed. "I feel so crazy not knowing."

"Lots of people who have been abused have fragmented memories. Things come back a bit at a time, when you can handle them. But also the details may not come back, and you have to trust your feelings."

"But I want to know!"

"Of course you do. You have to be patient. We're beginning to understand this thing with Post-Traumatic Stress Disorder. People with PTSD often don't remember things—they block out memories in order to survive. One good thing is that you are not alone in this. Other people have similar experiences—the feelings invade their lives but they don't have photographic images."

I sighed and settled back a little. I had heard of PTSD but did not know much about it. It helped a little to have a name for what was happening, giving it more reality. At the same time I didn't want to be just a category.

I WENT TO A LOCAL BOOKSTORE and stepped sideways along the shelves, looking out of the corner of my eye to find the "self-help" section and see whether the books on abuse were there. Checking

Writing About What is Not There

If you tell, I'll kill you, some remember.
Others, the creak of the stairs
some, less than that.
The importance of fog.
Where it is dense, things live
that must not be known
on penalty of losing everything.
Their reality my reality.
If they said *forget it*
who would be my Oprah
put the microphone in my face?
To keep family, I had to break
my reality
into fragments
hide the pieces
under the closet door
at the end of the hallway.
How could I face them in the mornings
eat my corn flakes and milk
if I recalled the nights?
How could I receive the love
that was given
sure as the whiskers
growing on his face,
the tiredness in her eyes
if I remembered?

around to make sure there was no one I knew browsing in the store, I reached for *The Courage to Heal*.

My heart would not slow down. I bent my head down and thumbed through, but it looked way beyond me. My vague feelings were mentioned in the first five pages of that book, but the rest seemed to be about having "real memories" and dealing with them. I didn't know that later editions of the book dealt with recovered memories. I needed stories of other people like me.

"HERE'S THE THING THAT really kills me," I said to Marianne. We had just finished eating dinner in her kitchen and were sipping tea. "It's the not knowing."

"Not knowing what?" she asked.

"Sometimes I don't think anything happened at all. Then sometimes I feel in my guts that somebody... molested me, but was it Jack?"

"Who else do you think it could be? A neighbor, an uncle?

I paused, stomach churning. "No, not really. Nobody visited our house. And... it just feels like family, some way I can't explain. My grandfather was a really creepy old man, but... I don't know!"

"Well, what about Jack? I really don't know much about him in spite of knowing you all these years. Are there clues in the kind of man he was?"

"He was... an odd man." I was having trouble ordering my tumbling thoughts. "Did I ever tell you about his affairs?"

"No! I'd remember that."

"I didn't consciously know about them until I was in college, when Kathy was five. I was home for Christmas vacation. Myra and I were in the living room. This was after they moved to suburbia. She told me Jack was having an affair with the woman who lived next door to his shop, Mrs. Robertson."

"That took nerve! What did Myra do?"

"She tried to get me to give her advice, was the first thing. That felt strange. I was only twenty. Then she threw him out of the house."

"Good for her!"

"But then took him back after a few weeks. I don't know why. I was back at college, thank god. It went on for years, and he was somehow involved with the Robertson family, too."

"Years! Why did she tolerate it?" Marianne wouldn't have put up with anything like that.

"She... I don't know, I guess she didn't feel she had a choice."

"But you said affairs, plural."

"The other one we knew about..."

"We?"

"Kathy knew about Mrs. Robertson, too, even though she was little. And then as she was growing up, Jack was involved for a long time with an alcoholic named Roxanne. She would call our home when she needed to get bailed out—literally, sometimes, bailed from jail.

"And then much later, when we were going through my father's papers after he went into the nursing home, we found a letter to him from Myra. It looked like her younger handwriting, and she was telling him off about an involvement with a woman named Betty. We were shocked, but I have to say, not too surprised."

"He was a turkey," Marianne said. "I think this tells you a lot about what he might do—his lack of boundaries."

"Yeah, I guess so." I took a sip of tea and thought about it. "I remembered this other thing, when I was a teenager, maybe fifteen. Jack and I went on a trip somewhere, just the two of us. It might have been to visit family in Maryland. On the way back home, we stopped for the night at a motel along Route 1. I remember we walked into a tiny office with a knotty pine counter. The middle-aged woman behind the counter asked what we needed.

"Jack said, 'I need a room for me and my daughter.' I could see the woman sizing us up. I was really startled, seeing she was wondering whether this was really a father and daughter. Then she said, 'You'll need two beds, of course.' Jack said, 'No, one bed is fine.'"

"What?!"

"Yeah, that's what I felt."

"Did you think he wanted to have sex with you?" she asked.

"No, really, not that."

"Were you thinking of how you'd been molested?"

"No, not at all. That was completely buried by then. It just felt wr..."

"Wrong! Inappropriate. Creepy. That's evidence."

"But evidence of what?"

"You're not going to find a taped confession. I think you have to go with what you have and the kind of person he was."

≈ 7 What Would It Be Like?

I COULD SENSE MY VOICE rising as I talked about my mother. Sarah reached for the pad of paper next to her chair and scribbled some notes. "She works so hard to deny her feelings," I said. "There is all that pain about my sister Suzie and about my father's unfaithfulness, and she just tries to keep on doing things, keeping busy. I feel so cut off from her."

Sarah asked, "Can you imagine what it would be like to be cared for the way you really want? Can you picture it?"

I felt my mouth twisting with pain and sadness.

"I can see that stirs up feelings," she said.

I could only sidle up to the thought, then my mind veered away. The lack was so huge that I could barely imagine what it would be like to have this thing called "caring."

One dark winter evening I pushed back the clutter on the kitchen table, spread out my journal, and asked "What do you need, child?" The writing started out sputtering but became clearer as I went on.

What would it be like to be cared for? Myra's rules of living (be strong, don't rely on anyone, be dependable and loyal) are posted in my being and mostly I don't notice them—they seem obvious.

Discontent. The prickling of pain at the back of my eyes that alerts me to sadness. And what is this sadness anchored to? I can't hope or expect my relationship with Myra to change. It is what it is.

I need holding, just holding and knowing. I need holding with no words. I need to be allowed to be exhausted and needy and limp and small.

I get an image of being something quite shapeless, like the blob of life before it is licked into shape by the Great Being. Image that—being just a blob, but so loved and cared for by the Great Being that I am slowly licked into my shape.

THE NEXT TIME I WENT to visit my mother, I got pulled off center again. Later as I sat in Sarah's office with the winter twilight pressing in through the windows, I told her about the visit. "But I also feel like there is a core of me that is genuinely strong and confident."

"Sit with that," she said.

I did, and I felt a solidity in my torso and gut, a kind of weightiness that was calm and ready, able to be present and not frantic. "When I was with my mother, I was able to do a lot of things for her without feeling crazed, but then she always asked for one more thing."

"What was that like?"

I told Sarah how I had been doing chores all Saturday afternoon. Finally I had said, "I need a break. I'm going to take a short walk."

"Oh, before you go could you just take these rags down to the basement?" Myra asked.

"Sure," I said shortly.

"Oh, and while you're there could you look around and see whether there are any signs of mice? I'm worried they might be back."

I sighed a took a deep breath. "OK, but then I get my walk."

After I told Sarah about this incident, I said, "It seemed like she almost couldn't stand having me be confident and clear, like she needed to push at me until I got off balance, too."

"She sounds unhappy."

"Well, if she needs me to be as unhappy as she is, I can sort of understand it. Her life is so constricted, it would be hard to have a daughter who is confident and knows what she wants."

"I suspect she also wants the best for you."

"That's true," I sighed.

> *Sadness. Myra has lived her life—it's not going to change. I wish: for directness, for her to be able to say, "I want...." I am mourning for what we did not and do not have. It is true that she was in too much pain to nourish my core being.*
>
> *Her life looks so shriveled to me, dried up and twisted by the lack of care and love.*

Myra developed macular degeneration—she was going blind. My heart went out in pity as I watched a warbler flitting through the spring branches. I wanted so desperately to appreciate and love her, despite all the evidence that I couldn't get through to her. And I couldn't separate my need to love her from my need to be loved by her when I was small.

Because I knew that Myra loved me the best she could—perhaps the best love of her life, as Sarah suggested later—it was hard to tear myself away from that hook.

MOTHER NATURE WAS my best model for love during these first years of recovery. Being in the out-of-doors filled me then, as now, with wonder and often joy. The indifference of the natural world gave me space to have big feelings and not feel rejected or scorned. I could hug a tree and cry on its bark and not be told to stop sniveling or get busy. And in the turning of the seasons and the cycle of growth—much larger than me—I felt continual hope.

> *The clouds—always the same and never the same. We have no words soft enough to say how they are always returning, always coming back but never exactly. The words have hard edges.*
>
> *And what if I never?*

What if I never shape that shadow into a picture with things in it?

What if I never find words to name and place and identify?

Then still these clouds walk from horizon to horizon, gray here and rhythmically steel blue there to the left, these same clouds or other clouds.

They are not lost, they come again, never the same, always the same.

Even if I never.

Occasionally I got flashes of another way to live, one in which I was not always being hard on myself.

The idea that I'm worth cherishing even when I'm not struggling with something— there's a thought! What would it be like to value myself? Live ordinarily, not in major pain? I don't know if I'm ready for that, but there are hints.

SLOWLY, SLOWLY I BEGAN to build a trusting relationship with the child inside, the girl I once had been. Little Jane needed to learn to trust my adult self, just as I needed to learn to take care of her. As I saw her more vividly, I knew that a little girl of three years old, who had been abused and betrayed, would not readily talk to any grownup that called her.

I set aside time every morning before work to sit with her, but she didn't always come. I might get a glimpse of someone with her back to me, or maybe a formless emotion. It was hard to trust that these wisps were worth taking seriously. I wondered whether this "little girl" was just a metaphor for parts of myself, but the process worked better when I took it literally and somewhat magically.

One morning in early spring of the year after Revelation Day, I set my kitchen timer to ring after twenty minutes. I sat in the rocker facing my big living room window but I closed my eyes to the cloudy day.

Where are you, little one? Oh, I should Xerox those handouts before class. I hope I have time to finish reading that student paper before our meeting.

No, no—back to the little one. Dear one, what do you need?

I remember another student who is depressed who will come see me today. Is there anything I can do for her?

No, back to my inner child, not hers. I see a little girl run and hide in the corner. Are you OK, little one? Can I come there?

No, I don't want you to come close.

All right, I'll just sit and you can come closer if you want.

I start to feel sad. I reach for the Kleenex and the tears fall down.

Sadness becomes sorrow. Baffling, deep, elusive, no anchor to it, a floating cloud that I breathe in and breathe out. But I want to be happy! I want to see and enjoy the world. And what I have is the weight on my eyelids, pain at the back of my throat, constriction in my neck.

I have what I have. Can I soften and allow the cloud of feeling to go freely through me, can I stand it willingly? Not to solve or dissolve it but to say, "Welcome. So this is what it is now." I sit with it, sort of. It's hard to sit with—always any thought or image or sleepiness is preferable to really staying with it.

Even while I responded to my inner child's profound neediness, I was overwhelmed and scared by it, but I did not turn to Sarah. How could I possibly let myself depend on her? I could sense how vulnerable that would make me and it made me feel very, very small, as if a single word could wipe me out. One morning the emotions were physical.

My face needs contact. It is hard to admit the depths of my need. I want to be babied. I'm so afraid that if I reveal it, I will be rejected, unloved, repulsed.

Lonely. This child. This yearning is so deep—is there any end? Is there ever any peace? Yet it is good to allow my yearning to fill me. It is a relief to come to something after wandering.

Sarah often asked, "How does your little girl feel right now?" Having someone inquire from the outside made it much easier to feel the process was real. And she was hugely patient, saying, "Take your time. Just sit and see what comes." She was willing to listen to the faint, faint stirrings and hints. She did not seem to think they were "silly" or trivial. Her patient belief helped the little girl directly and helped my adult self to sit and listen. It served as a role model for how I could parent myself.

Often we spent time in silence as I felt my way through the layers. In one particular session in April, I filled Sarah in on the happenings in my life and then she said, "Would you like to sit and go inside?"

I settled in and closed my eyes, breathing deeply. I felt a vague, huge sadness. Unclarity. "All I get is murkiness. Nothing is clear."

"Stay with that, if you can."

I stayed a long time sitting with that light purple haze, feeling as if it were endless; nothing would ever be clear. "I'm beginning to get a sense of Myra guarding the door, telling me to keep busy and ignore my confusing feelings."

"All right. Stay with it."

"Oh, this little girl, she's only three or four, so small. She's the refugee girl from that photograph. She is a dear, dear girl and she needs me to hold her. Now she is in my lap and I am caressing her hair. She is such a delight."

"That's right. I'm glad she came. You were patient."

MY FRIEND PAM was one of the people I'd told about my suspected abuse. She instantly believed me. The second time we were talking about it, she said, "It really happens. I know somebody at work who remembers being raped by her father and her uncle when she was young, and beaten, too."

She meant to support me, but I got a sinking feeling. How could I take seriously what happened to me, when it was so minor compared to that story? My family was not that awful. I didn't know what to say to Pam, but I took my reactions back home with me.

> *It wasn't such a bad childhood—decent really, except for the pain of Suzie, Myra's depression, Jack's unfaithfulness, and maybe the X factor. How do other people walk around in the world?*

I have to laugh and shake my head now, looking at those words, "decent, really, except for the pain of Suzie, Myra's depression, Jack's unfaithfulness…." The family configuration was not set up for happiness, even before the possible abuse. "The X factor"—I still could not firmly name it sexual abuse.

How could I understand what had happened? I borrowed Sarah's copy of Judith Herman's book, *Father-Daughter Incest*. It seemed dated and referred to older victims who remembered details of the abuse.

> *I feel I want something that speaks to the earliness, the vagueness, the victim's smallness, and the bewilderment of a small one who could not understand. The utter disparity of size and power. The shadowy feeling of it. The uncertainty. The slow process.*

Some things rang true in the book: mothers who were distant and often debilitated by depression or other causes. Also she named clearly the fathers' assumption of privilege, just like Jack.

"SARAH, WHY CAN'T I seem to find friends who want to be close and share? Last weekend, I really felt bad on Friday and Saturday night with no one to be with."

"Did you spend good time with your little girl?"

"Yes, I took a long hike one day. And I spent time drawing. But what about other relationships? I feel like I don't have enough contact."

"The most important relationship is between you and the little girl." Her brown eyes were intent as she looked compassionately at me. "That is the one to focus on now, and others will follow."

It felt paradoxical to be instructed to go inwards when I wanted more social contact and human relationships. But I wasn't satisfied with superficial relations and I got easily frustrated in social situations where people were chatting. Anyway, it seemed like the only thing I could do, so I spent a good bit of time by myself.

"I DON'T KNOW where I'm going. Right now I just don't want to focus at all," I said to Sarah as the April rain pattered on the window.

"All right—go with it."

I closed my eyes and went into the space that was calling me. It was a vague and drifty place I was backing into, unseeing but deliberate. No clarity. No images, no words. Just space with a heavy heart, eyes of tears.

I could sense the child there in this indeterminate space and I said aloud, "I'm asking her, 'What about it?' I'm not going to press her about what happened." I could feel the child inside feeling completely confused.

"I don't understand," I said out loud to Sarah in a child-voice. Suddenly I was small and I had shoes with hard leather soles and I scuffed my shoes on the carpet sideways, toes pointed in. My legs were short and I wore white cotton socks. "I don't understand."

The adult Jane just sat next to Little Jane, no words.

After a while I lost the vividness and slowly, slowly floated up, staying with a drifty feeling. "It was really important to say out loud that I don't understand."

"I know. You made space for the child to say that. It is very confusing for the little girl, and it is important to let her speak."

Memorial Day weekend. I feel I should be with people, but need solitude. I decided to take a day of solitude and silence. The little girl is scared I will desert her in the next six weeks.

I was in another busy period in my life in the world. While on sabbatical, I was working with a colleague to organize a conference at the college and co-edit a book that would arise from the conference. In one six-week period I had two out-of-town meetings to attend, a week-long workshop to give, the conference to host, and things to write. We got the big grant that I had written. It was a perfect time to have another revelation.

Deeper

≈ 8 The Big Ugly

I WHIRLED IN THE non-stop world of work, running a conference here, attending one there, dashing on to the next event. While touching down for a few days between, I had therapy on a Thursday afternoon. Following intuition, I had reserved a dance studio for an hour's solo time just before my session.

I entered the light, airy studio space with a sense of disquiet. Putting my things on a wooden bench, I changed to my dance pants and began a slow series of stretches on the skin-smooth wooden floor, under the tall windows with their fill of tree branches. I loved the feeling of pressure on my joints and muscles as I slowly melted into the floor, then pushed off it. The floor has always been one of my favorite places.

Suddenly I was overtaken by a heart-stopping bodily sensation. Where did this overwhelming feeling come from? How did it get to invade me? I writhed on the floor, trying to find my way back to the present reality. Deeply shaken, I got up and walked around the perimeter of the simple room, attempting to regain the sensations of normality and safety.

I packed up my things and went on to see Sarah. As I waited in her quiet office, I heard my own shallow breathing. When we started talking, I did not want to return to the sensations that had ambushed me. "I just was in the studio before I came, and I had a really weird feeling that felt yucky and secret."

"Oh?"

"Yes, really awful. But I really don't want to deal with it now. I have this conference to go to in a few days where I have to be really professional and give workshops. Can you help me put it away somehow?"

"Do you want to put it in a box or something like that? That works for some people. I can understand why you might not want to deal with it right now."

I tried to sense whether that idea would help. "Yes, let me try a wooden box with a lid and a lock, someplace where I can put it and it can't get out. I'll put the box on a shelf in a cave, and I'll come back to it when I have more space." I sat visualizing the safe, strong box for a minute or two.

"I want to tell you about this conference that I was leading. I felt really triumphal about it but I didn't have much of anybody to share it with."

"Great. I'd love to hear."

"We organized it very well, I thought, and had lots of group activities to get everyone engaged. The participants liked one another's ideas.... It was actually fun! But when I tried to tell the women's group about it, they didn't give me much space. I started to talk and then another woman interrupted to complain about her work situation."

"Mmm, that can happen. That group doesn't seem to be working too well for you. But you get space here to rejoice." I spent several more minutes taking credit for a job well done. When we hugged goodbye, I knew I would not see Sarah for a couple of weeks because I was traveling for work.

THE BODY-MEMORY KEPT expanding inside me, calling out its importance to my unwilling consciousness. I was afraid to give it reality even by writing it down in my journal. Although I had tried to put it away in a box in a dark cave, the feeling would not go away.

I created a new place to write about it, at the back of my notebook, inside a border of solid lines, a box to try to contain it. It was too shattering to put anywhere else.

Fragments in a safe box. No one sees this; I don't have to tell anyone this, please.

I'm rolling on the floor in the studio (by myself) and I open my mouth and make "Nnnnng" sounds and get a sensation of ((no no this is a very safe box elsewhere for the bad bad thoughts.)) big warm something, my mouth hot and full, darkness in my eyes, pressure all through my mouth and throat. I can't breathe, feel choked and nauseated. Oh my god, penis in my mouth. No no no please no. It couldn't be, I wasn't.... Nnnnnng,

(Male voice, justifying) "It's not like she was raped."

A few days later I put more things in this box at the back of my notebook:

Here we can talk about it as if...

Is it possible? Surely not. Surely my father wouldn't, no one would do that with such a little girl. Surely I would remember—surely I wouldn't. Now we're talking about oral sex and also about something with my genitals! Is this possible? It is possible, people do these things. Surely I wouldn't have grown so strong and big if that happened? Surely I could have. People do.

But to the little girl I say—yes, it is possible; it is amazing what people will do. You're very brave to be talking with me about this. We can talk "as if"— that's fine and helps keep it safe.

I was overwhelmed by this new form of memory. I did not have any idea that there could be such a vivid and overpowering body-memory without a place or a time or people. I also did not know how to ask Sarah for help with it—and besides, I was afraid that if I talked to her about it, it would become more real and I couldn't escape it.

Why is it that I'm keeping things to myself and not telling Sarah? Don't I trust her? I do. Mostly. I think that keeping things to myself is the way I learned to be safe, so I cling to it.

But the memory would not stay in the box.

silent girl

in my body
the silent girl
no mouth
just a place where

the silent girl
it's a blank
just a place where
my neck tightens

it's a blank
I am in the city
my neck tightens
can't open my eyes

I am in the city
there is no location
can't open my eyes
which way is up

there is no location
underwater
which way is up
can't stop thrashing

underwater
mouth closed
can't stop thrashing
no smile in the picture

mouth closed
you have the right
no smile in the picture
to remain silent

you have the right
no mouth
to remain silent
in my body

> *This is hard. Not quite as bad as the initial, "Oh my God," but really hard. I had a nice brunch with my son and his girlfriend, then went shopping. Driving home alone, I'm putting my hand to my mouth, gagging and crying hard. Oh my God. No. No. No.*

My son was staying with me for a few days. In the mornings he slept in while I sat with Little Jane in my bedroom with the door closed, crying and rocking.

While I was eating breakfast with Will one day, I looked at this quiet young man whom I loved so well, and I wanted to connect with him. I took a shaky breath and said, "I'm having a hard time with some early memories."

I must have looked stricken. He came over, towering above my chair, and held out an arm to hug me. "Sorry about that." I was comforted by his genuine concern.

I called my friend Marianne and visited with her before leaving for an education conference in North Carolina. She greeted me at the front door in her shorts and a halter, saying, "I've been gardening. I hope you don't mind." After she hugged me she led me back to the kitchen of her wonderful Victorian house, with its ancient gas stove, where she brewed me a cup of tea.

I blurted out the mouth-memory that had overtaken me. Sobbing, I said, "I still can't believe it. It's so awful So yucky."

Marianne said very gently, "You look like you need to be held." She stroked my head and invited me to lie on her living room rug while she held me and I cried. I got no hint of doubt from her and she didn't ask me to be more specific than I could be. She kept saying, "That's terrible." Her acceptance of my gush of feelings, which felt to me like a break-down, paradoxically helped me feel strong and competent.

At the education conference I ran two workshops in four days and attended numerous sessions. The place was packed with well-meaning, animated science teachers. Intermittently, I kept getting very intrusive feelings of gagging, having my mouth stuffed full, and nausea. I could keep up the professional façade for a couple of hours at a time, but then the urgent, physical feelings came at me and I was swallowing and swallowing, afraid and unable to think. I retreated to my tiny, hot dorm room for hours each day and lay on the floor sobbing under the big floor fan.

After a couple of days of this, I wrote a letter to Sarah, telling her about the body-memory, and adding, "I feel like I'm grieving. I don't know what I'm grieving. But it's a huge gaping hole, an earthquake rearranging my continents, a loss of ground. I am here crying with shock and loss. I don't feel outrage (yet) or anger—it's shock and sadness."

≈ 9 Trust You?

ON A BREEZY AFTERNOON in early July I sat on Sarah's couch staring at the potted plants in front of her patio door, feeling miserable. I was intensely vulnerable from the mouth-memory that had come two weeks before. Although I had written to Sarah about it, I was not yet ready to speak of it aloud, and she was letting me take my own time in coming to that point. And I'd been having furious debates inside myself:

> *I feel rage—don't talk to me about support and people! Where have you been all my life? Don't talk to me about support unless you want to step in and hold me. Don't preach at me. Don't tell me what I should do. People don't come through for me.*
>
> *I start to feel crazy again when I deal with this. I feel like Sarah has opened this up as a problem: Jane not acting correctly so that people don't give her what she needs. It must be Jane who is wrong and making herself lonely. What's wrong with Jane? It makes me furious.*

I think of telling Sarah about my anger and fear of craziness, and I am frightened. I fear that if she doesn't go away and be cold (oh my yes—tears, recognition, that's like Myra), if she doesn't go away, I am afraid she will exact a payment—that I see myself as wrong/crazy and take up her view and her scheme for my improvement (is this what Myra did? I start to blank—thoughts are unthinkable).

What I said to Sarah was different. "I wonder how to guard myself better; these feelings are so overwhelming. I just walk around feeling raw."

"Are there people you can call on for help?"

"Well, there's Pam, the old friend I dance with every few weeks. I guess I could go and cry on her shoulder, but she talks so much. It's hard just to be there and be miserable because her needs take over. And besides, I don't know if I want to go into it fully with her. I don't know if that feels right."

"How about Marianne, you said she was really helpful before."

"Yes, but she's so busy...." The more Sarah gave me suggestions and advice on getting help, the more resistance I felt, and then I felt like I must be bad for not being able to get the help. It seemed like there was something fundamentally wrong with me, if I couldn't get the support I needed.

"Is it possible," she asked, "that you gravitate towards people who can't give you what you need?"

"What do you mean?" I was sobbing and angry. "It really sounds like you think it's all my fault!" I felt abandoned, not in the least bit able to see that it was the little girl in me who felt that way, just consumed by the misery of it.

Finally, towards the end of the session she said, "If you want somebody to be here while you cry, I'm here. I can sit with you and hold you."

Something in my stomach let loose and dropped—such a relief. "That's it. That is really what I was looking for. I need that." As soon as she said she'd hold me, I could see that I was wanting all along to say, "I'm vulnerable—take care of me." But it was too hard to reveal my need.

Just as I left, she said, "You can call me anytime, really. It is all right to ask for help. I'll be here for you." It sounded good, it was good, it helped, but it was a long time before I could believe it deeply.

Doubt

Doubt tiptoes through my spirit like a thief
picks away at my hems,
splits my fingernails.
Courage makes darting runs at it
swooping down from the top corners of the room
but maybe humility is the one
to save the day, simply saying
this is what I can do.

Even now, six years later as I work on this writing, my eyes start to prickle and I feel a vague fear around my heart. I need to sit with the little girl who is scared. I write one page and then Little Jane cries. I hold her and say, *I hear you—it was really scary, and there was no one when you were little who believed you and would hold you. All those years from when you were little, it felt the same way. But things have changed, little one. Look how they've changed—now we have Sarah to depend on, we have many friends who see and believe you, we have an audience waiting in the writing group and elsewhere, hoping to see more of you.*

At the time when I most needed to trust someone, it was perhaps harder than ever. My mother had pushed me away when I was young—how could I trust Sarah now? It was impossible to believe that someone could really be nurturing and non-judgmental.

> *Transference? Wanting the good mother? Sure, why not! At the same time, this feels like an illicit desire, asking too much, wanting to go back and be a child when I should be a grownup. Will you take care of me? Can you hear me? Will anyone be tender with all the places where it hurts?*
>
> *I feel like a lovesick person petitioning Sarah for attention. What is she inviting me to do when she says, "You can call on me for help"?*

In the midst of this intensity, I led a workshop on teaching and creativity. About thirty engineers gathered at round tables in the evening of a humid July day. Most of them didn't know one another and I could see them sizing each other up. They were good people but they would play power games if given the opportunity.

I was inwardly smiling as I implemented my plan. I told them to gather in groups of four and exchange information about themselves and their work for about fifteen minutes. Then each of them was required to introduce a new acquaintance to the entire group. It was gratifying to see how the usual "I'm so important" introductions were transformed into generous offerings: "I want you to meet Jaime Y from San Jose State. He is implementing an amazing freshman seminar in which all the students design software to solve traffic problems in the city."

IT WAS A RAINY July day two weeks after the session in which I felt so vulnerable but could not see a way to go. Sarah came in late, again, as I sat and waited tensely. I still had not told her in full the terrible body-memory about my mouth.

"I've been thinking about the last time I saw you..."

"Yes?"

"I know I asked for help in being less vulnerable and then I," squirming slightly, "I couldn't take any help, everything you said, I resisted."

"Uh-huh," in a neutral tone.

"I think maybe I wanted to be more vulnerable, not less. I think I want to trust you more. I know that sounds strange, I mean, after all this time, how could I even question it?"

"Do you know if there are particular things you want from me?"

Taking deep breaths, I gulped, hesitated, felt very small. "I'd like to have you hold me, but I don't know if it's OK to ask."

"That is all right. I can sit with you sometimes, if it will help."

"Oh, wow, that is exciting. But it's scary, too."

"Can you say more about the scary part?" she asked.

Silence and my heart was beating hard. "I'm afraid I'm going to depend on you too much. I'm going to lose my self. I know I want you to be the good mother I didn't have. You and I have always worked with a certain separation and I'm afraid of losing that. I am afraid of losing the sense of who's who."

A short silence. "It's OK. It is all right to be lost for a while and feel like a baby and be protected. You need to go back through the stages of growth, but your self is strong and you will come out the other side."

"I guess I get what you mean..."

"It's all part of the process—you lose the separateness and then you get it back later."

"I guess I see, sort of. I like the idea of you holding me, but I have to ask you—can you hold me and still keep separate? Because I can't do that part, I'm afraid I'll be lost and swallowed up. I won't know who I am."

"Yes," she said firmly, "I can definitely stay separate when I hold you. I will remain conscious and grown up—you don't have to worry about that. I can sit with you and hold you and still keep the sense of who is who. That's part of my job. I will only touch you in ways that are safe, and you can say 'no' any time."

"Really? Oh." Sigh, and my stomach relaxed. My shoulders dropped something they had been carrying for the longest time, and my eyes streamed tears of relief.

Looking at this scene now, I see I was also afraid that she wouldn't be able to keep safe boundaries with me. I feared that loving touch would somehow become violating touch, although I could not allow myself even to think of that.

"I'm giving myself credit for being brave," I continued after I had cried a while.

Sarah asked me to sit with that and I did sit quietly, honoring my work in speaking for the child. "I opened up a path she couldn't take then because it wasn't available. When I was young I was thoroughly cut off. Any time I tried to be held and believed, it was stamped on."

"That's true."

"But my little girl inside always had the capability of being direct and clear."

"I believe she was always there."

I took in her words and held them.

After therapy I keep smiling and crying. How interesting that Sarah and I worked for so long with me taking care of myself, and now she senses it's OK for me to be taken care of. To be a baby.

From Myra I got no separation and no support-love. How marvelous to imagine getting both. The path that was cut off. A chance to go back.

About to enter the Tunnel of Transference.

I wanted Sarah to be perfect—perfectly available, perfectly understanding—so I could trust her. She kept reminding me that I had to tell her what I needed. A part of me wanted her to know it all intuitively, so I could be an infant and not have to ask. Asking involves risk.

Sarah was not always available, and small lapses felt like gaping craters in the earth.

Sarah, where are you? "Depend on me," she says and then she's gone. I call and leave a message and she doesn't return my call. An inner voice says, "There's no use getting upset about it. Nothing you can do, no use wanting it if you're not going to get it." I notice that even when I wish upon a star, I wish for something reasonable so I won't be disappointed.

Could I possibly really take a chance on wanting? Take a chance on loving? Take a chance on needing and depending? Close to tears but no release. Only glimpses and hints—afraid to be angry, afraid to be too sad. Little girl in limbo, in a no-feeling state. Is there any slightest chance I could show Sarah my anger and sadness at her?

It took years of patience and work until I could say fairly easily to Sarah, "My little girl got really upset when you were late. I got angry. I felt like you'd never be there."

And Sarah would reply quietly, patiently, "I can see why you are angry. It's hard when I am late and you don't know if I'm coming. I'm sorry."

So simple, so basic. But without a background of trust, I felt like I wasn't allowed to be angry. My ordinary emotions often made me feel nuts. While I was dwelling in this very tender place of trying to learn to trust, the "real world" did not stop its demands.

≈ 10 Get Out!

GREAT NEWS! The big grant that I had written in the previous autumn came through, more than a million dollars over four years for my department. It gave me a lot of responsibility for disbursing and overseeing the funds. Since I was known as a tough woman, no one thought twice of pushing for what they wanted, whether their approach was direct or sidelong.

In August I declared vacation for a week, but I was on campus for a dance workshop in a different area of the campus. On the sidewalk outside the dance building, I ran into a colleague. He greeted me cordially and then launched,

"I know you're on vacation, so I can't ask you..."

"Yes, I am loving being away."

"...but I just wanted to let you know that I want money to go on this trip to the West Coast with a student, and we need some funds for the supplies for the analytical machines, and there's another thing..."

"No, not now," I interrupted. "Monday. Right now I am on vacation."

"I'll come find you on Monday."

Some faculty, men in particular, seemed to have no trouble asking for anything they wanted regardless of the terms and purpose of the grant. They would corner me in my office or in the hall and talk on and on about what they wanted and why. Even though I had written the proposal clearly to delineate what activities were included, some people didn't seem to care about boundaries. Externally, I coped all right with it, but inside I felt I was faking being an adult.

Doing the inner work about the abuse, while being professional on the outside, left me feeling I was between two worlds, possessed by demons.

> *The pain is not a physical but a whole body-mind-soul pain. Panic. Get out! Someone protect me! Don't let this happen to me! I'm helpless to stop it. I know you'll get your way.*
>
> *Imagine, the administrator of the million dollar grant is a little girl with her father's penis in her mouth. Is a victim who could be taken advantage of with no recourse?*

Leaving work, I would dash to my car, mouth full of ancient feelings, eyes brimming. All the way home I cried and talked to my inner child, trying to convince her that the world was not really so unsafe.

Now I recognize those incidents as flashbacks—pressure in my mouth, nausea, the feeling of being overwhelmed. Viet Nam vets get flashbacks of limbs flying, explosions, and voices. I got the choking and panic that were the scariest feelings to the little girl to whom it happened. Therapists call that aspect of PTSD "intrusive symptoms." They were intrusive, all right, the literal feeling of something intruding into my mouth. They also were intrusive in that I could not control when they came up. I could try to forget, try to put that ugly stuff into another compartment, but I was not very good at it. It seemed like the only way out was through.

Unless I really was crazy, and that was not the view of those around me, then these intrusive symptoms were trying to tell me something.

The memory itself was bad enough, although I did not trust it enough to call it a memory. It remained just as invasive and disgusting over the next weeks. Even worse, it stirred up a swarm of other feelings: mistrust, doubt, lack of boundaries, confusion, and shame. It brought back the way life was in my family, with whispered conversations, isolation, fear of craziness, and fear of telling. The flood of different issues makes sense as I write this, but back then it just seemed like more overwhelming, chaotic "stuff."

It felt crazy when I thought I was the only one having such strong surges of feeling. But later I realized that other people were acting a good deal crazier than I. Grown men threw temper tantrums in the halls if they didn't get exactly the lab space they wanted. Women threw snit-fits in other ways. Faculty were acting as though they still were two years old, or four at most. What they perhaps lacked was awareness that they were being ruled by the needy little kids inside them. I knew it vividly in myself.

I REARRANGED THE CHAIRS in my office and brought in a couple of extra ones to accommodate the crowd. In a fit of nerves, I had cleaned off the table and moved the piles of papers to my desk. One by one, the other four faculty members filed in and chatted.

"So this is brand-new," I said, as I opened the meeting. "With the new grant money, we need to be sure it's spent fairly among the faculty members. We need to set up clear guidelines. I think we need application procedures."

"Oh, I don't know if we need to be that formal," one woman said.

"I think it's a good idea to be transparent about it," I answered. And it was. I felt saner. I was the chair of the committee and had considerable clout, but it was no longer me against the world. Faculty members gradually learned to respect the rules.

From inside the storm of frightening feelings, I began to see how my department at work resembled my birth family. There wasn't much overt emotion. Behind closed doors, we female faculty complained about the gender roles where men did "important" things like research while the women took care of the students. And always there was the threat of male anger.

Perhaps the deepest, subtlest reminder of my family at work was the "objective" world-view: facts are what matter. My department was less hard-nosed than many science departments, I know, but the pervasive skepticism about the softer sides of human existence meant that I had to keep a lot of myself out of sight. Faculty were eager to change the subject when personal feelings were mentioned. I remember a colleague looming in my office door, telling me he was worried about his daughter. He rolled his eyes as he said, "Her college roommate claims she was sexually abused. She's just upsetting my daughter and taking up space."

≈ 11 Crazy?

It's so weird to have another world that comes through like a bad science-fiction novel. This world that seems so unbelievable enters my mind all the time. I want it there, I want to be with it, but I don't. I want to spend all my time there. But I don't—I want relief in other things.

Surely it's not possible he did that to me. If I grew up OK, then it must not have happened. If I'm not OK, then I'm untrustworthy, I'm crazy.

As I opened the door to Sarah's office, I carried the weight of doubt below my ribs and in my mouth. She opened the inner door looking happy, saying, "Beautiful day!"

"Yes, but I'm in a mess."

"What's up?" she asked, settling herself in her chair and picking up her pad of paper. "Tell me."

"It feels horrible to walk around doubting myself all the time like this!"

"Can you describe the doubts more?"

"I don't believe he could have done that, not my father."

"Do you have any other ideas? A neighbor?"

"No, it just doesn't feel like that.... My grandfather was creepy, but we hardly ever saw him—oh, I just don't know!"

"We know something happened," she said firmly. My throat relaxed a bit.

"But how could I grow up looking normal if that happened to me?"

"It's amazing what people walk around with."

"But I should remember something clear, shouldn't I?"

"Not necessarily. You had good reason for blocking it out. For survival."

"And this physical memory—there's no way on earth I could have made it up. It's too huge and immediate. If I made something up, it would have more details!"

"I think that's very true."

There was more, but I was getting a desperate urgency inside, a breath-holding feeling, wanting to burst out. I exploded into tears and wails, howling, moaning, grabbing handful after handful of Kleenex from the box beside me. A little girl desperate with need.

Sarah sat quietly opposite me. "Remember to breathe," she said once.

"Could you come and hold me?" I asked, when I could get my breath. She sat beside me, her arm around my shoulder and holding my hand. Feeling a welcoming shoulder, I collapsed into another stream of tears.

"I think I need to tell you about the feelings I got in the studio, the body-memory I wrote you about."

"You're right. I think it's good to tell me in person."

"I... it's so hard," I gasped.

"Take your time."

"It feels like something big stuffed into my mouth. I can't breathe, I'm choking."

"Breathe slowly now."

I inhaled, and blew out a gust. "I can't see anything, there's no place, no time, just this feeling."

"Uh-huh."

"Do you believe me?" I panted.

"I believe you."

"No, really—do you?"

"Yes, I do. People don't make these things up for fun."

I asked her at least four different ways, and she answered with firm confidence. She kept her arm around me and stroked me like a small child, as I gradually whimpered into calm. The feeling of craziness that gripped from the inside like a huge spider was gone. Some place in my belly relaxed in an unfamiliar way.

I asked, "It really is possible?"

"Yes, it really is possible. People do these things, unfortunately."

After I was quieter, Sarah returned to her familiar chair.

"I'm really not crazy?"

"No, far from it. You were not the one doing the bad things, but you had to take on the wrongness in order to survive, back then." She paused and seemed to search for words. "Because you weren't in a position to put the blame where it belonged, on the grownups. You had to structure your whole personality to accommodate that wrongness."

After all this time. All this time. I waited until I was ready.

Later that day. My knees are happy with the shock of it. My tears are grateful and smoking. Someone believes me! She has seen my dark and pitiful places, she has heard my fear and she believes me! I don't have to hide.

I SAT IN THE QUIET room at our next session, noticing the psychology books in the bookcase and the birds outside the window before I plunged into my emotions.

"But all I have is this *feeling*! I can't remember anything else."

"What else do you want to remember?" she asked sympathetically.

"Anything concrete, a place, a time."

"These memories often come in fragments. That's how it happens for many people."

"But I don't know how old I was or anything. I think I was six or seven, but I have no real way of knowing it. I don't have any *pictures*. Will it ever get clearer?"

"It might, or it might not. It's not necessary to have pictures; many people who have been abused as kids never get clear memories. What's important is being with the feelings about it."

"But it's so hard."

You demons

I am calling you out.
You with the name All Or None
with the foul breath and arrogant air.
Nothing less than the full risk will do
you always say.
I call you Jump Off The Bridge.
Your lopsided sneer shows yellow teeth
one eye squints down your warty nose
while an eyebrow arches in disdain.
You are permanently more radical, more daring.
Next to the railing you chant *jump, jump, jump!*
And besides, your companion murmurs,
it's not such a big deal, you've hardly done anything.
This one named Looks Trivial To Me
expert at minimizing, whittling,
peering through the wrong end of telescopes.

Today I call you out.
I want to know who is brave?
you cold-skinned, slimy squinters
or the silent girl who takes the key and descends
step by step, turn by turn
going into profoundest darkness
trailing her hand along the damp wall for guidance
leading without knowing where.
Who has courage? You, jeering by the bridge
as your shriek makes her cower?
She pauses then goes on.

Finally she calls out for help
dislodges another screamer from the wall
name of Do It Alone.
You all flap around her head
like rabid umbrellas,
proud of your effect on her.
And she goes on.
I ask you, gods, who is brave?

"Yes, it is hard, not being clear. The murkiness is one of the hardest parts." Sarah drew in a breath, looking thoughtful. "But you may have some clues in the family structure."

"Yeah, Jack's affairs, Myra's passivity.... Oh, I just don't know." I fell silent, confusion blanketing my mind. Then I remembered another incident.

"There was this time when I was walking home from school for lunch. I remember it was sunny. As I walked past the Callahan's house next door, two dogs were playing in the yard. They each had one end of a stick and they were playing and growling. I ran down the side steps and into my father's shop to tell him, all excited, 'Two dogs are playing tug-of-war, over in the Callahan's yard!' He said, 'Are you sure it's tug-of-war?' 'Yes, yes!' I said.

"He looked at me and he said, 'Maybe they are mating and got locked together. When I was young there used to be cruises in the Baltimore harbor, and some of them were at night. Couples would go on the cruises to be romantic. They would get very passionate, and sometimes the spotlight would sweep over them...'

"Inside, I was going *What? What?* But he just went on.

"'The spotlight would sweep over, and the poor couples would panic and get locked together right in the act. Maybe that's what is happening with the dogs.'"

Sarah looked shocked. "He said that?"

I blew out a breath. "Yes. All my joy was gone. I remember that one of the shop guys, Oscar, was in the room. He started making horrified faces and small gestures in the corner where he was. I could see that he didn't think Jack should be saying this to me, but maybe he didn't know how to speak up to the boss. But having Oscar there, that did something for me. Someone else saw that what Jack was saying was out of place."

"For sure it was out of place. He had no regard for you. He was only thinking of himself. How old were you?"

"It had to be fifth or sixth grade, when I walked home past that house. It was so weird." I sat in silence for a while, crying and taking little gasps. I wanted to ask again, but it was too hard; my heart was thumping and my throat was tight. *I shouldn't have to ask again. She already said she believes me, that should be enough. She'll just get impatient and angry with me.* "Do you believe me?"

"Yes, I believe you. And you can ask me over and over. Think of how long you learned not to ask and not to tell."

She believed me! Then I cried a gusher of relief.

When I attempted to read books about sexual abuse and recovery, they often triggered cascades of shame, confusion, and even loneliness. Partly it was the intensity of all those stories, and partly it was because I seldom found accounts of recovered memories.

Jennifer Freyd's *Betrayal Trauma: The Logic of Forgetting Childhood Abuse* helped the most in understanding how my memory of abuse could have been hidden so long. She says that closeness to the abuser actually requires children to repress memory in order to stay within the family system. How could the child remember the father's abuse and still remain dependent on him for her life and sustenance? In her logical, cognitive argument Freyd tells about studies of reported abuse showing that children often forgot for years, even if they had been taken to the emergency room. The closer the relationship to the perpetrator, the more likely it was the child would forget for some period of time.

To our next session, I brought Sarah my favorite picture from my childhood. It was my first-grade picture, the kind that was snapped in two minutes by a professional who came and took photos of all the kids. Black and white. A little girl with two long dark braids disappearing down her back, a tidy part in the middle of her hair. I remembered the dress, yellow cotton with brown plaid trim and puffy little sleeves. Myra had ironed it into crispness.

"Oh, look at her!" Sarah said. "So dear, trying so hard. Look at that mouth firmly closed. She is not smiling!"

"No, it looks like she was told to smile, but she's not. See, there's one corner of her mouth down-turned and disappointed but that other corner turned up like it's trying?"

"I see. She's trying hard. Her eyebrows are so straight and solemn. Those eyes, they really get to me—so shiny and pleading. Her shoulders are hunched up like she's carrying the world."

"I always was such a good girl. I tried so hard. I want to thank that Good Girl for working to keep it all together."

"I know you did. I can see it."

"Good Girl, you did so well, getting good grades and being obedient and trying to stay connected to Myra and Jack the best you could. You did your very best."

"And Good Girl is still around—she's inside you."

"For sure! I'm still far too conscientious." I laughed.

I took the picture in my hands and studied that small, vulnerable face. "Now, that is a picture of after, isn't it?" I asked Sarah.

"Oh, yes. Look at those eyes. They know far too much."

"So I guess we can be pretty sure that the abuse happened by first grade."

"It looks that way. This is not a happy girl. I just want to hug her."

It is hard work, this writing—scraping the keel right down to the wood. I took a walk just now on this gray day, a bit cool and moist. Sat on the pebbled shore by the big reservoir and watched the waves roll in.

No wonder Little Jane felt crazy. What he did made no sense, was terrifying, overwhelming, and indescribable. Then Myra commanded her to act normal and ignore it, so she couldn't tell or be comforted. All the craziness that was out there went inside.

≈ 12 Witness

I HAD BEEN LOOKING forward eagerly to participating in a week-long movement workshop, but I didn't see how I could bring the disgusting mouth-memory with me. If the point of Authentic Movement is to be witnessed being oneself, how could this self be acceptable?

We met in a huge studio on a remote part of my own college campus. The room was oddly industrial: clammy gray plastic floor, pipes and ducts in shiny metal above, a warehouse roof high overhead. But with our cushions and mats and a wonderful vase of wildflowers that our organizers brought, we began to make the space our own. There was a large circle of about twenty people sitting on the floor and I greeted several people I knew. We started by going around the circle saying our names, giving a movement gesture, and saying why we were there.

I am not feeling safe or at home in the workshop. I hope I'll be OK. In the big circle I didn't want to tell about myself and so I just said, "I'm here for renewal." I feel fragile.

After those introductions we did a meditative walk in the woods, with one of the leaders ringing a bell occasionally to invite us to stop and notice all around us. I was deeply moved by the shapes of the pine bark—big scabby flakes in wonderful shapes that looked like islands or topographical maps. Suddenly I saw: it's in the cracks between these tough bark scales that the tree is growing, so tender and thin a skin. This was the image I shared when we were invited to speak.

In the evening we began the movement sessions. Meeting again in the big gray room, we sat in a circle and received the guidelines for safety, confidentiality, and structure. This time we could move or witness at any time during the forty-five minutes. Our leaders would witness the whole time, and only they would speak in response to our movement, if we asked them to. So I knew that Rita and Peter, whom I trusted, would be watching, but anyone else could also see.

I entered standing, put my hands to my face and felt myself sinking into a hole. I exited soon, screaming internally—Rita, Peter, notice my pain! I went in again crawling, stayed very low.

My mouth, my mouth, I can't reveal it. Stuffed my hands into and around my mouth a dozen ways. Kept my face down mostly and hid turtle-like. I rocked. Some sounds got past my mouth— that felt good. A very hard place to be. Hard to be seen. Hard to be unseen. I can't move much. Huddle, huddle, huddle. Protect. Finally I did raise my head up a little, rocked in the protection of my hands, on my elbows and knees, body all hunched up. The movement felt new, with a little excitement but no sense of safety yet.

After the moving, we gathered in small groups, each with a leader, and had a few minutes for each mover to speak about her moving. I glanced at the waiting faces, then looked down at the floor and said, "I've been uncovering some early stuff that is so painful I can't show it. I literally can't show my face. I moved the whole time with my hand covering my mouth. I didn't expect it to be this hard. I don't know how much I can bring here."

I was thinking that I hadn't moved in public since these mouth-memories came, not with anyone. I felt like I was the sick one, the weakling. I hated being this needy.

In the next morning's movement session, I crouched again on the floor.

Promise

I promise, you will be
terrified. On edge.
Beyond reach but right here.
Utterly in this moment. Exposed
on the tightrope, naked.
Willing to have this happen.
Your guts sinking with fear and
with the weight of your truth. Nausea
later, for now the certainty that you
are following a truth
to the tips of its nerve endings.
You are allowing yourself to be seen.
Trusting in
this actual self to be visible,
as you are.
I promise, you can do it.

I cover my mouth the whole, whole time. Protecting that mouth? Declaring the place of hurt? It is about being here while at the same time I am a small girl, at the same time being the one who protects her.

I get up and walk around, still with my hand over my mouth. Around me I hear people moving, someone crying. It is a lot just to be here with these people and carry this secret openly. I feel the nausea when it comes, feel the breath when it moves through, the sound that cleanses my throat and makes space for me.

Take time, take time, take time. If I don't yet act out fear and rage, then know: this is already a huge piece of work. By simply being here and holding true, I am "going for the jugular," as Natalie Goldberg put it. Not to force it—I've had that, thank you very much. Now I am going gently.

I felt shame, afraid everyone would see what had happened to me. Afterwards as we were sitting on the floor in our circle, I told my witnesses that I had been working with early, very difficult memories. They did not know about my shame and its cause, but they said things like, "It looked like a hard place to be," and "When I imagined doing those movements, I felt vulnerable."

It was extremely important to me to be seen and accepted while I was in those humiliated, secret places. My pain did not overwhelm or repulse the watchers. I still feel it a miracle, as someone who learned that she needed to be cheerful and keep quiet about the abuse in order to keep the family together. I could both show myself and not be forced to explain.

Gradually, different qualities and states started to emerge during the week of the workshop.

Walking, jiggling becomes energy—hands and arms fanning energy into me, a blur beyond control, a quickness running through me. It's mine, it's mine. He didn't take it away from me, taint it forever; this pounding, breathing energy is mine. My mouth is open and uncovered and powerful, making my noises.

I got glimpses of serenity and connection to larger forces in the universe.

I am standing, arms wide open, feet apart, making swishing sounds of the wind with each in-breath and out-breath. I am in a desert landscape with the divine wind blowing through me, my breath joining with the world. Spareness, unity, life in a landscape. I have peace and love in knowing and caring for. Caring for my face, my mouth, touching my own skin softly.

And then the flashbacks come: nausea, swallowing, gagging. I can allow it to happen somewhat.

The structures of world—wind, touch, breath, sound—all there to support that little cradle of pain, suffocation, and bewilderment. All there to support the child in rebuilding her innocence.

When we sat in a circle afterwards, I reported that I had felt a divine breath blow through me in the desert. Authentic Movement practice assumes that the mover's experience is primary and only she can say what it means. Witnesses can speak of their images and projections, but they are just that—the watcher's experiences. What a delight and learning this is for the child whose truth was erased: now my subjective knowledge is my truth, and no one can tell me otherwise!

In this case a woman who had witnessed said, "Oh, in my imagination you were under the sea and barely withstanding the sweeping currents." That was her projection reflecting something going on in her psyche; my image was still of strength and deserts. Yet I was touched that she saw huge natural forces affecting me.

At lunchtime one day, I went for a walk and saw Queen Anne's lace—all those tiny blossoms and the minuscule dark red dot in the center! Look how the complex bud unfolds into the white lace. Then when the blooming is done, it curls up again, differently, in order to make its seeds. Who could invent a miracle like that? My eyes had been washed by all those tears and now I could see again.

≈ 13 Hiding

THE WORD "SACRED" drifts through. On a mission, a mythical heroic journey. Yes. Why not? I got a lot of books by Jung out of the library. He did that—saw life as a sacred journey. Standing on the threshold, I feel that some of this journey is individual and some of it is larger than my singular self.

Occasionally I glimpsed this larger sense of journey. But mostly the work went painfully slowly.

One hot August day in therapy I told Sarah about the events of my week and then she said, "Why don't you just close your eyes, sit quietly and see what comes?" I sighed and went quiet, then peeked. I could see her eyes closed, too. That felt fine, as if she inhabited the same unseeing, intimate space I was in. In the quiet office I could hear her breathing.

I felt a familiar sensation of sinking, my flesh settling slightly on my frame, my belly letting go, a flow downwards in my back. I floated down in water, deeper. I saw myself in the space beneath the roots of a tree in a swamp.

Everything happened slowly. Time was elastic. The small could become large. Little by little, I was learning to allow bits and pieces to emerge from this dream-state—fragments and nonsense, images, gestures. At first I censored them, thinking, "Oh, that's nothing." But then I began to trust that each might lead somewhere and deserved an airing, coming as they did from some unconscious place. I began to see this trance-work as a skill, although my scientist-self, my father's daughter, was still skeptical.

This day I drifted, hoping for a hint of direction. I didn't want to speak and break my own spell. Nothing happened.

Finally I said, "I'm just feeling lost. I don't see anything."

"That's all right. Try to stay with it and breathe."

"Nothing. I feel loster than lost. Where am I? Why don't I have any feelings at all?"

"Keep with it, if you can."

"I feel like there's a wall around me, and I'm not going to let anyone in." I glimpsed a gray stone wall.

"Uh huh."

"But part of me wants to get through to the little girl. I want to be with her."

"Do you know why she has a wall?"

With eyes closed I saw her—a little girl sitting with her arms around her knees, ignoring the grownups. "Oh, I see, little one. You needed that wall so much. It kept you a little bit safe. You had to do whatever you could to keep safe, and that wall helped a lot."

"She was doing the best she could. I believe she did well to make the wall."

"I honor you for being so strong and putting up the wall. You were smart and strong and brave to do that. It helped you survive."

> *Oh Stubborn One! I see you with your back to me, mouth closed tightly, lips set. You're not looking happy. Oh Stubborn One, let me sing a praise song to you. Let me sing of your determination, of your pride, of your strength, of your ability to keep yourself separate.*
>
> *The Stubborn One says: I am alone, I am clear, I am firm. This is what I do, only knowing the clear and definite things.*
>
> *Oh Stubborn One, I see you with your back to me and I am baffled. I wonder where I have lost my connection to you. Oh*

Stubborn One, I sing to you. I try to tell you it's OK, I want you to trust me. You still sit there having none of it. Stubborn One, only clear facts for you, only denial of shadows.

The Stubborn One says: It's all OK, I'll take care of it, I can do it, I can be by myself, I can do it just like this.

Oh Stubborn One, fifty years of being clear

fifty years of being definite

fifty years of No, I can do it myself

fifty years of I'm OK

fifty years of not trusting anyone at all.

Not. Trusting. Any. One. At. All.

Although I honored this Stubborn Girl, I was still impatient when my inner child would not speak. I wanted to be able to be together with her often. I did not understand what lived behind the wall.

Lost

≈ 14 After

what he did and my remembering

ambush
mistrust hopelessness

wasteland all colors of ugliness

fog of indescribable dimensions
dense as dirt elusive as air

rage at invaders those who cross boundaries

then more smoking ruins
collateral damage

remains of attempted conversation

communications cables
mangled and sparking.

≈ 15 In the Fog

I was being tumbled by the surf, or swirled down a long tube, but there was no surf, no tube. My skull was turning, or my brain inside the skull, or my mind inside the brain, turning and turning. My breath came short and shallow. My awareness felt completely separate in a white-out blizzard. My mind got loose from my body. I didn't feel my shoulders tensing. I didn't feel my breathing. My fingers lost sensation. My lips buzzed with numbness as if they were cold. The world narrowed so there was only the inside whirling, nothing else.

Without changing, it changed. I was not whirling, I was standing in the fog, on the fog. Nothing moved. There was a slight purple tint to the fog. I knew that the fog went on forever in every direction. I would never get out of there. Dimly I knew that Sarah was in the room and that I was sitting. I could have broken out of this no-place if I willed it, but I needed to stay. Speaking was a foreign concept—all concepts were foreign. It took enormous effort to open my mouth. Words were hauled up by bucket from far away, buckets full of little tags to stick on snowdrifts of vagueness.

It was a muggy August day two months after the Big Ugly memory, coolish and damp in Sarah's office.

I had said to her, "I really am appreciating the way you hold me lightly, I mean how you give me care and attention without making me trapped or smothered. I am amazed at this process. It feels so special to me."

She looked at me with affection. "Well, you are doing fine with it."

"I kind of want to ask where I might...." *Whoosh*!

I have before me The Void—purple gray, soft, murky, lusterless, empty. It's scary, unknown, so empty. Nothing concrete. I can't see or feel a thing. And as I am frightened, I feel stuff at the back of my throat. Dizziness. It's hard to stay here.

I slowly let the words come to describe it to Sarah. Then I surfaced a little to ask, "What do I do?"

"You can stay with it or you can ask about that feeling in the throat."

"I'll stay with the Void. Little Jane offered this to me—this is where I should stay. It feels important to be patient with it."

It was seductive. I went deeper and deeper inside. "Little girl, how did you hide this place? Where did it go when you grew up? How did you get on in the world?"

Slowly and reluctantly I thought about returning. "Where is this place? So far away. I thought dissociation was just to get away from bad unbearable stuff, but this seems close to good places."

"Say more about that?"

"It seems like a state I get into when I'm dancing, like a trance state. I feel like it borders on a huge creative unconscious space. It's really seductive."

Sarah seemed doubtful. "You may have created that place in order to be protected and try to make yourself safe."

"But it seems like more than that, more positive."

"I'm sure it has its good qualities," she said carefully.

THE WINDOWS WERE OPEN to the late-summer breeze and the cricket sounds when the women's group met at my house on a Sunday night. They arrived together and helped themselves to fizzy water before sitting in a rough circle in my assortment of chairs and sofas.

My interactions with the group had felt unsatisfying. Sarah said that in her experience, women's groups go deeper as time goes on, but mine seemed to be getting shallower, at least for the kind of emotional issues I was having. Did that mean I was doing something wrong? Did I have the wrong needs? I was thinking about leaving the group. Time went on. In the two months since the mouth-memory, I still had not told the group about it. I knew I needed to take the risk.

In the check-in I said that I wanted time to talk about my work on early issues.

"You know I've been working on these childhood issues," I told them. "A couple of months ago I got this physical memory, this feeling of something stuffed in my mouth." I told them that it felt overwhelming and disgusting. And that I still didn't have visual memories, just the sensations, over and over.

"I know that I was young when it happened and I didn't have words for it." As I talked to the group, I breathed deeply and looked down, focusing on speaking truthfully. "I'd really like responses. I especially need to hear that you are here with me, that you heard what I said, and that you believe me."

Alice said, "I know what you mean. In my therapy I had to go back to child-places that brought up tremendous, just tremendous anxiety for me. It's important not to push it too far, to go at your own pace."

"When you talk about being sexually abused," Grace asked, "does it bring up shame for you?"

"Well, for me it's more a fear of being crazy. I am afraid I am wrong and crazy."

"Anyway, I know it's really hard stuff. I hope you'll be patient and go easy on yourself."

"I think you're really brave to be doing this," Deborah said. "Really brave. Does it make it hard to be with your family?"

"Kind of. It makes me understand why I get so very outraged at Myra's helplessness. You know, when she can't decide whether to have French cut or regular string beans." Everybody laughed; they had heard many stories of my frustrations at her home.

I still felt jittery. They had sounded supportive, but nobody had addressed my naked need to be believed.

After a short silence, I took courage in hand and said, "I need to hear directly from you that you believe me. It's like talking to a very little, literal child." Each woman did say she believed me, and they were moved by it, I could see. They hugged me. And some of them said it was valuable to them to see and hear this powerful work. I felt both glad and vulnerable.

Self-doubt

like razor wire: the slightest touch draws blood,
like blackberries: the thorns cling and pierce,
like garbage: the smell clings to me,
like an old family friend
whom I don't like but
who is made to feel at home,
a corrosive acid that eats silently away,
a bleach that takes away colors.
A crow eating roadkill.

I drove north on Interstate 91 singing the spiritual "Oh sinner man" at the top of my lungs along with the reggae version blaring out of my CD player. "Oh sinner man, where you goin' to run to?" made me grin, imagining my father running but not being able to hide, even after death. I was on my way to a solo backpacking trip in Vermont's Green Mountains.

This is the first time I've taken these "new selves" camping. As with mourning, it seems to take a year to move through the cycle. I see friends, I do work, I visit family, I go camping. I do all these things with my new knowledge.

I yearned for solitude and felt safe among the thick trunks of the trees. On this trip I shunned people and casual conversation, spending my days hiking. At night, I stayed in the open shelters along the trail, hoping I would not be joined by other hikers.

I was led to this place of quiet. Thank you, long-dead tree with barkless trunk, pale twisted grain and lichen, whose trunk I sit on. Thank you. Silence in the air except for insect hums and a bird's chirp. Thank you, carpet of oxalis and moss, surrounding me with jewels of green leaves, repeating, repeating, repeating your message: grow, grow to your own height, flourish in the sun and rain and cloud. Thank you.

I breathe silence. I listen to the earth's breath.

How sweetly the earth hummocks over corpses of trees. The stone bones of earth are only a few feet down under. The calm gray green color of dead tree, the six feet that are left of it, top fallen away long ago. Quiet, slowing, noticing.

When I came down from the mountains and then stepped out of the car to get coffee, I felt I was on wheels, so smooth and easy. I had spent the last night alone at a trail shelter with rain pattering down peacefully.

"Sarah, I talked to my women's group, and I asked them…." I felt dizziness whirling me. "Oh, the fog again."

Sarah said, "Go with it."

So I dropped the story and went to nowhere. I stayed there a very long time, perhaps 20 minutes.

A nothingness so vague it goes on forever: No thing. Nothing. Everywhere. No colors, just kind of gray-white. Nothing here at all, in all directions. For all time. It will never change. I will never get out of here. No feelings. Nothing.

Amazing! Just when I said there was no feeling at all, a tear leaks out from each eye. The feeling of the tears burning their way down my cheeks—a miracle! I'm sobbing but gently. Not to be comforted either, not yet. Just this amazing happening of the tears, the only sensation there is. And sadness.

"I don't know how this relates to the abuse or why I need to do it," I said to Sarah. "But I know it feels important."

"You are doing it. It might be what Fritz Perls, who founded Gestalt therapy, used to call the Fertile Void—a place where things can arise."

"Yes! I keep feeling there's something in here for me. The vaguest place keeps yelling, 'I'm nothing! Nothing here. See! Nothing at all.'" We laughed at that, a moment of comic relief.

FOG. AND BEHIND the fog, another betrayal. It came to me on a hot afternoon as I sat writing at my kitchen table with the late-August sun pouring in.

Despite the cluttered kitchen all around me, fog crept into my eyes, my ears. It enveloped me in an eerie gray calm.

But what was beyond the fog? I asked Little Jane what was out there. "No one could believe me," she says. "Not possibly. It's no use talking."

Suddenly Myra's voice said, "What's done is done. You have to forget it. We're counting on you to be quiet."

"What's that?" I asked Little Jane. "Can you tell me more about what Myra said?"

Little Jane: Listen. Please listen.

Myra: You should forget, that's all you can do.

LJ: I need you to listen, I can't just forget—it's wrong!

M: Pretend it didn't happen. That's all I can do, give you this advice.

LJ: But I want you to listen and believe me. I need you. I can't pretend. I don't want to go away and find someone else. I love you. I want you to help me.

M: I can't help you. I'm doing the best I can.

LJ: It's lonely and scary, but if I have to, I'll find someone else to tell.

After the words poured out, I sat stunned and shaking. She told me to pretend to forget, just as I was supposed to pretend I did not have a sister Suzie. Myra's Betrayal.

I did not tell Sarah about this for several weeks. I held it all inside—fearing, perhaps, another betrayal.

≈ 16 Out-Raged

Driving down to see my mother that Labor Day weekend, a year after the initial revelation, I was flowing with the interstate traffic and muttering to myself. Just before I left, I had received a memo from my department chair, including the simple words, "I assume you will..." followed by extra work to do. He did not negotiate it with me. Since it concerned the grant I was heading, I figured I should have been consulted, not told what to do. Little Jane interpreted the situation to mean: I'll have to do it because he wants it. This time, my instinctive panic was overwhelmed by a rage reaction:

> *His assuming that I will mold to his wants and be convenient, obedient—that I will do his will. The rage is far beyond the provocation. That's OK.*

Somehow I negotiated the situation in the real world like an adult, not letting the rage boil out.

The next morning, I woke in the airy upstairs bedroom that had been my sister's when she was a teenager, the walls painted alternately green and yellow.

The despairing fog and gloom that is usual for Myra. It seems to me that it's her state of mind. But I am bewildered. Why, with this seeming outward OKness, do I get so bogged down and hopeless feeling? No purpose, no way, no life, no fear, no hope. Sounds a bit like the void, doesn't it?

During the days with my mother, spurts of anger erupted. Every time I did something for her, it seemed she asked for one more thing. "While you're down in the basement, would you look at the pipes?" "While you're out, would you stop at the liquor store?" They were all reasonable requests, especially since she could not get down the stairs to the basement, didn't drive and could not get to the liquor store. But it was never enough. She had no limits.

Rage accompanies me, its tide rises in my throat, gives me pictures of volcanic outpouring. Little Jane, it's OK to be enraged— even if it seems like there is no cause now, you have plenty of cause.

It is scary. I can't believe what a huge reservoir of rage is boiling in here. I'm amazed to hear myself sound calm and reasonable, while the beasts and children in me are roaming and screeching, screaming and jumping up and down. It takes my breath away.

No wonder I get so depressed and hopeless when I visit Myra. So much rage waiting. I've been afraid to notice it, unable to notice it for fear of an impossible explosion. I can't wait to go home.

When I thought about Jack instead of Myra, the reactions were even more visceral:

Rage! Waiting anger wants to chew, bite, sink my teeth into. Am I nuts? Am I bad for wanting to enjoy biting? Not me. He's bad, not me. Am I crazy for wanting to bite, bite, bite? I'm powerful and have a rage as huge as the world.

Will memories come back and flood me? Kill me? No. I'm in control now and you're dead. You are dead. Your dick is dead, your fingers are dead, your head is dead, all of you is dead and I am alive. I am alive and in control and my memo-

ries won't come back unless I say it's OK, and you won't come back at all.

Before going downstairs to breakfast at my mother's house, I drew in my big sketch book, large slashing scribbles in red, purple, and black. My arm zigzagged in violent, emphatic motion, my whole-body rage focused on the slender stick of oil pastel and its contact with the page. After the catharsis, I briefly imagined having someone rage on my behalf, someone to be angry for me, not helpless and weak.

I teetered between outward good-daughter behavior and my inner sea of anger.

MY FRIENDS HAD SAID they would arrive at my house at 7:30. It was a wonderful late-summer evening, warm and soft, and I was looking forward to an intimate evening of talk on my screened porch. School had started, but I had made time for a visit from two of my closest friends.

Chris and Sally were also dancers. After we attended the summer workshop together, we had spent many afternoons and evenings together learning about one another's lives, talking passionately about movement, emotions, and spirituality. We also met in the studio, moving and witnessing one another.

As the time ticked by, I became irritated, then furious. I had to work the next day—didn't they understand my time was worth something? At 8:15, they got out of the car, laughing.

"You're really late. I'm upset!"

"Ah, we just were eating and the time passed," Sally said.

"But I have to work tomorrow!"

They shrugged. No apology. I felt ripped off and jealous. Their casual response said it was uncool to be angry, especially about a trivial thing like time. I acted as if it was all right, but inwardly fumed. Was I wrong to be angry?

The next day, I was clear that I had to work it out. I didn't know whether I was risking our friendship. I picked up the phone, paced up and down in my living room, and talked with Chris.

"I was really angry when you and Sally came so late last night. You know, school is starting and I don't have a lot of time, and you just showed up really late without calling or anything."

"Oh, I didn't even notice. I was in a hassle with Sally and I really wasn't all there. I was feeling tense."

"Mmm, well, but I was really hurt."

"I'm sorry. I know I was distracted because I had this thing going on with her. But I can see why you're angry. We were just eating but we really should have kept track of time."

"Thanks for telling me what was happening. That helps."

She didn't have to grovel, I just needed an acknowledgment and a sense that my anger was accepted.

When I called Sally, it was not as simple.

"I was angry when you and Chris arrived so late last night. It's the beginning of the semester and my time is precious."

"I noticed you were angry when we walked in."

"Well, I hope you can treat my time a bit more respectfully, let me know if you are going to be late."

"I can't really promise to do that. I think I see time differently, more of a fluid thing."

I didn't hear any empathy in what she said. Sally was self-involved, always a-boil with her own crises. Sometimes I wondered why I was friends with her.

I still had not told Sarah about the vague voices in my head that said, "Forget it. Just pretend it didn't happen." They had come to me three weeks earlier.

We were running out of time in our session as I was talking about my rage at my department chair and how that reminded me of being forced by my father. Sarah said, "It sounds like your rage wasn't directed towards your mother."

Whoa! I felt. *It's like she pulled the plug—dread, no, wait! Stop! Not that! No, wait, stop, reel that by again!*

"It's more like I take it for granted. I am always angry at her helplessness and impotence around people. I was always mad at how she didn't notice my feelings. And her complicity." As I drove away I wondered, *Is Sarah trying to tell me that I wasn't angry at Myra? That I shouldn't be angry at her? That it wouldn't do any good?*

A few evenings later, I drew the blinds in my living room, closed my eyes and began to move slowly in dream-body time.

I saw a dragon's hind legs—massive, scaled blue-green—and huge tail. The tail was round and scaled and had spikes on top. The legs were spread wide like lizards' legs. A hint of the head—yes, that is where the fire would be. I began to cry with the power of it. The mouth of steely gums, leather lips, teeth pointed, conical.

This mouth was strong and hard like steel, like stone, the eyes like glass. I heard a sword grating on the scales, glancing off. The dragon of my vision was so strong and huge that it did not need to be aggressive; it could just breathe and people had to show respect. I could hunch alongside it and be protected utterly.

> *I am touching my own face, it is soft, so soft, too soft. And I live in this too-soft mortal hurt-able body. And I live here? I rock myself with pain and sadness. Where is anger? It seems so far away. Do I want to be this dragon? So hard! So hard, so hard. Do I want to be this person? So soft, too soft, no fire, all water, water and soft.*

Sometime in the next year, when I was visiting my mother's home, Kathy and I went through an old box of family jewelry. I picked up a silver ring, much tarnished, with two dragons on it. I polished it at once and have not needed to polish it again, because I wear it every day.

UNCOMFORTABLY, I PERCHED on the edge of the couch opposite Sarah. "I think I need to do some hard stuff, but I don't know where to begin," I said.

She invited, "Why don't you close your eyes and go inside, get in touch with the little girl?" The room became quiet.

> *I enter into the child's space. I enter a fog.*
>
> *The fog is everywhere, it is endless. I wander there. It is blue, violet gray, red. It goes on forever. I want to be there but I am hopeless. Nothing. Ever.*
>
> *I sense a little corner in the fog, a space for the little girl to hide.*

In the endless fog, finally I wanted to hear a human voice. I said to Sarah, "Would you ask me where I am?"

Sarah responded, "Where are you?"

"Remember how we ended last time? You said it sounded like I'm not angry at my mother."

"I remember."

"I've been working on that, and I have some really unclear memories."

"Oh?"

"I'm pretty sure I tried to tell Myra about what Jack did to me in my mouth."

"Do you have any idea how old you were?"

"I kind of feel it was around five or six, but I really don't know." I squirmed on the couch, frightened at not knowing.

"That's OK. You don't need to be clear."

"I feel really little and confused. My words won't come. I don't have any words to tell it. A big person is asking, 'What happened?' Over and over, she says sharply, 'What is it?! Tell me!'"

I was sobbing wildly. "It is too harsh! I need to be asked, 'How are you? How are you feeling?' I need to be held and comforted and believed. The question is too hard. It is too much." Shakily I reached for the Kleenex.

"I need much softer questions. I need to be angry at the questioner. I need to tell her, 'No, wait, listen! Listen to me!' I need to have my confusion and lack of words be OK. I need to be held and listened to." I could feel my lips, the little girl's lips, trembling and tender. Words were not coming easily.

"Your mother didn't listen to you. She asked you grown-up questions but she did not really listen to you respectfully."

"'What happened?' is a grown-up question. I needed her to ask, 'How do you feel?' 'What can I do for you?' I needed her to hold me."

"You were very little. You needed more understanding."

"And then she said," I gulped for air, "'pretend it never happened. It's best to forget about it. Nothing can be done. What's done is done.'"

"Oh no." Sarah's eyes were filled with concern.

"She crushed my knowledge and my memories to pieces. It seemed so reasonable, and she was the grownup."

"Awful. That was wrong."

"Yeah, but what can I do with it?"

"Maybe you want to talk to her about it here. You could put her in that chair over there and tell her what you need to say."

I swallowed and blew my nose, then shifted slightly to face the wooden rocking chair. "You didn't hear me, you asked me hard questions. You didn't listen. You told me, 'Forget about it. Pretend it didn't happen.'" I was panting, exhilarated at my daring, but scared.

"You had your pain and fear so strong that it held me and kept me from telling," I told the Myra-figure in the rocking chair. "I get the fog again when I get close to where you told me to forget. You told me."

It was clear for a few moments, then I said, "I don't know, I don't know. Everything is confusion."

Sarah said, "I believe you. You are doing fine."

I heaved my chest up in a breath, then started again speaking to the chair.

"I don't know exactly what you said but I know you, I know exactly what you said. I can't recall your face saying it to me, it's all in pieces. But I know exactly what you said to me to make this fog close in and keep me. Your denial was so reasonable, so 'right,' such a correct thing to do.

"I'm still not done, but I don't know what to do," I said to Sarah.

"Do you want to try being Myra?" Sarah asked.

I blew out a breath. "Phew, that's hard. But yes, I guess so."

I moved over to sit in the rocking chair. I could feel my shoulders shift and something inside realign as I imagined myself being Myra, with a daughter who had just come to me extremely upset. I felt helpless, with all the baggage of a troubled marriage. I had no idea how to cope with this little girl's pain and confusion. I was frightened and paralyzed. "You have to forget it," I said hopelessly. "That's all you can do. It's done with. You have to go on."

I moved back to the couch and became the little girl again. "But... but. Why won't you listen?"

"I can't," I said from the rocking chair, frozen. "I don't know what to do. I really can't listen to you. It's too hard." I felt panicked, convinced there was nothing I could do. Then I couldn't stand to carry it any further, and I returned to the couch.

I turned back to Sarah, "Wow, that was hard. It makes sense, but it's still tenuous. None of it feels clear to me—or do I know, but I feel doubt? Surely I don't mean it that she didn't listen? Surely I don't mean she didn't protect me?"

"I believe you. These memories often come back in pieces, blurry. I believe you."

"She didn't hear me! She didn't listen. She wasn't there to hear me the way I needed to tell her! It might be that she protected me by stopping him, but she didn't tell me that she did. She told me to forget it. She acted from her fear. It was the best she could do and it wasn't enough."

"I agree, it was not enough."

"She betrayed me! It was a second betrayal and then there was no one left!"

"It's true. Then you didn't have anyone to go to, no one safe."

I turned back toward the invisible woman. "Myra, I see your pain and shame reaching way back into your past. I see your fear keeping you from listening, keeping you from being strong. I see it. I feel it. You have to go away now. You have to go away so I can talk and feel. I'm still angry at you but I give up on you. You're going. I need to be away from you so I can remember.

"Sarah, I have to turn away from her. I can't tell my stories with her there. She has to go."

"Good idea. Do you want to tell her that again?"

"Go away! I have somebody to listen to me now. You need to get out of my head!"

I left Sarah's office reeling with feelings, thrilled by her careful, respectful attention, exhausted from the little girl's fear and intensity. As often, I went to take a walk in the woods, bringing my journal.

> *I sense a new grownup inside me who listens and gives space. "We have all the time. I'm here, I'm listening. You can tell anything you want, or draw, or just have me hold you. I know it will take a while for you to believe me, of course. But I'm here and strong enough to hear. It really will be different now."*
>
> *Can I really believe that I am—abandoning—Myra? That I am putting her aside and taking care of me?*

THE NEXT THURSDAY was a beautiful early fall day. I parked my car, walked down the driveway, and stepped down the little path to Sarah's side door. I took a deep breath and went inside. A loud whooshing noise. Sarah opened the inner door and said, "Oh, I'm so sorry. I tried to get you at your office and home."

"What? What about?"

"I can't meet today. My washer sprung a hose leak and it's all over the basement. That noise is the vacuum handling the water."

"Oh no. What now?" We made an appointment for Saturday morning.

I felt I should be grateful that Sarah had made time for me on a weekend. I tried to bring myself to be present at our Saturday session, but it was like hauling a sack of rocks. In response to her questions, I kept saying, "I don't know."

"Are you upset at me for not being here on Thursday?"

"I guess so, but I can't really feel it.."

Back at home I wrote overlapping layers of words in different colors in my big sketch pad.

I don't know why this is such a fragile time.

"I don't know" means I know.

This is not a good time to let me down.

Last week I told my mother to go away.

Where are you? I depend on you.

Do you hear me?

This is what I know how to do—I hide to let you know I am hurt and angry.

As I huddled through the rain for my next appointment with Sarah, I carried these feelings inside my coat.

"I was really upset with you last week, when you cancelled at the last minute."

"I can imagine so."

"I think I need to do something with the feelings."

"OK."

"Let me sit quietly and see." I went inside. It was too quiet in there. "I feel something inside, could be anger, maybe."

"Stay with it, if you can."

I stayed. It felt too hard to speak. First a lot of silence inside, then feelings bumping big, like rocks in a torrent. My eyes were squeezed shut. *Can I really say these things and she won't get angry at me? It's too hard. I can't risk it, but I have to.*

"I had just gotten rid of her, of my mother, I moved her aside and was just making a safe space."

I opened my eyes and saw the concern on Sarah's face.

"And then you weren't there. The safe space is… I need it so much, this space. I need it clear. Taking care of others is out. My space, mine. Where I'm taken care of."

"Let me know if I can do something to help."

I went quiet for a minute, then took a big breath. "How about if I tell you I'm angry and you say you're sorry?"

"All right," she said calmly.

I watched her face carefully. She didn't look frightened or angry. "I needed you and you weren't here! I needed you to help me make this space. You weren't here. I'm angry about that."

She was silent, taking it in. I felt it was all right to say more.

"I don't want to be reasonable and grown up. I don't want to be nice! I needed you and you weren't here!"

"I'm sorry," she said slowly. "I am sorry that I wasn't there when you needed me." And I believed her.

"I can be angry even if you don't like it, even if you are hurt. Even if you don't like it and you are hurt or angry. I'm entitled to it. This is me."

"Indeed, you are entitled to be angry."

Something in my chest let go of its clench. *This is amazing—it actually feels resolved! Imagine that.*

≈ 17 A Turn

I INTENDED TO WRITE about all of my second year of work on the abuse, as I have written about the first. But it turned out that I could not. I reread my journals of that time, a four-inch stack of spiral-bound notebooks with dense scribbling almost every day. I flagged the passages that were important, little post-its in bright colors, with notes like, "I dream that I have to take care of an old man and get him out of the house before the house falls down," and "Hypervigilance, I have to be alert all the time at work."

Then the big sketchbooks. The spiky drawings of rage kept coming. Slashes of red and black, jagged zigzags of thick oil pastel, filled up page after page. They filled my need to express with muscle and eye, flesh and bone, then sigh, *Yes, that feels like It.*

Extra-large sketchbooks contained chalk pastel drawings of flesh—immense, tender, disturbing bodyscapes. Pink and glowing. I remember how I did them, laying the groundwork with layers and layers of rubbed white, then pale pink, then deeper pink. Smooth and tactile, loving. It was disturbing the way they evoked fingers rubbing on young, blameless flesh. Lines of pink and red formed edges, making me gasp with their suggestions of buttocks, of violated boundaries.

Working on these pink drawings, I felt shame and something more—the feeling of being there "in the flesh" and being the temptation. I felt I was a part of what he did—not running away, not screaming. I was a participant in the family system that held it all. I had a terrible feeling of complicity.

Dozens of drawings were all vagueness, clouds of subtlety with no clear center. The eye could not focus, the mind could not grip. All was fog, in uneasy shades of yellow-green and lavender, or glowing light yellow or pink, or despairing gray of denial and nothingness.

Again I prowled the "recovery" section of the local bookstore. This time I bought *I Never Told Anyone*, edited by Ellen Bass and Louise Thornton, hoping to find stories like mine—vague ones, ones in pieces. This book only had well-remembered stories, but it had an introduction in which Ellen Bass talked about patterns of abuse. I was stunned to read that girls are often blamed for their supposed seductiveness, even if they are only three or four years old. The abusers rationalize their own "innocence" by claiming that they couldn't help it, they were carried away, it's in men's nature to find girls irresistibly attractive. That passage rang an old bell.

I went to see Sarah on a summer afternoon, two years after the initial revelation. Her patio doors were open to a soft breeze. I told her about the book and then, "I can remember Jack telling me about men's needs. He said that men have a biological need for sex, a really strong drive. That they can't control themselves."

"How old do you think you were?"

"I guess I was twelve or so. I was old enough to know what sex was. We were in the shop in the back room with all the parts bins, and nobody else was around."

"Do you think he was warning you, so as to protect you from other men?"

"Uh-uh. It didn't feel like that, not protective. It felt more like he was telling me the way he thought he was. He believed in a kind of turn-of-the-century Darwinism, with a lot about instincts. He said that women 'get men started' and once men get started, they can't stop." It made me hurt inside to remember it.

"That's a lousy excuse," she said.

"Yeah—a way to avoid being a grownup."

I WAS IN MY OFFICE typing at the computer when Harry came to the doorway. I swiveled my chair to look at him. "There's this great opportunity to analyze soil samples," he said. "The students are eager to get going on it. Can't you just release some funds now, and I'll apply for something later?" I knew that Harry was sincere and an excellent teacher who attracted students into research.

"The committee," I said, "You need to apply through the regular procedure."

"But we want to start in two weeks. I don't see why you can't..." He came closer, still talking. He was very tall.

I stood up, not knowing quite why, but now I see, not wanting to be sitting with my face just below his belt buckle. "The committee. It's not my decision." *That's exactly why I set it up this way,* I thought in the dim back of my brain. *So it's not a matter of your pressuring me to get what you assume you deserve to have.*

When he left I sat back down heavily, my mouth feeling stuffed full and my stomach twisting bile-green. *Breathe,* I thought. *Breathe. Remember it's not the same now. It's not like that. I have the power now, not him.*

It took me a while to understand that these flashbacks were just as real as those of a war veteran. Maybe it's the movies, or reading novels where the character gets whisked into a detailed re-living of a scene, that made me expect photographic, clear scenes. Or maybe it's the word "flashback" that fooled me into thinking of scenes where "it all comes back."

I started to read research, when I could bear it, bit by bit. One of the hallmarks of post-traumatic stress disorder is the fragmentation of memory. Some pieces only come back as physical memories, or fragments in different senses like smell, touch, hearing.

I'm not alone in having only fragments. For a veteran it might be the instinctive dive under the table in response to a loud noise. For an abuse survivor, it can be the pressure in the mouth, nausea, an ache low in the belly, or fear in situations that seem ordinary but are obscurely threatening.

BUT THIS IS THE YEAR I am not going to tell in full. I tried to write about it but experienced total writer's block. Something was getting in the way.

I went to see Sarah. She had read all the chapters up until now. Besides being the therapist in the story, she was still my therapist in daily, in weekly, life. I sat looking at the sunlight filtering through the hemlocks outside her window.

"I don't understand what's happening with the writing now. I feel so good about developing this system for working—reading the journals, making notes, staying with it until the mess forms into themes. I can name the themes for this part if I have to—flashbacks, flesh, innocence or complicity, rage, lots of fog—but I somehow can't get my mind around them. It's not ready."

"Well, that's OK, there's no rush."

"But I've been with it for months. It's never been quite like this before. I have all the material but somehow I can't go there."

"I wonder who inside is having trouble," she said.

"I don't know. Maybe I need a dialogue."

A little silence. "How about if you invite all the little girls into a circle—Good Girl and Stubborn Girl and the sad little one and all. Then see what needs to be known."

"OK." I squirmed a little on the couch and then sat quietly, letting the image form in my mind of the circle of Big Jane and each of the little girls. It hardly took any time before a voice came through my mouth saying, "I don't want to go there! I don't want to! It's too ugly, it's too yucky! I don't want to!"

I asked Sarah to sit beside me and hold the hand of this distressed girl, and she did.

"I don't want to go back! How many times do I have to go there?"

Sarah paused. "That's a really good question, It's different for everybody, but there does come a time when it's enough. You stop going back and you go on."

"Oh." I felt the reverberations of her statement. "Maybe it is that time for me. Not that the issues are gone, but I don't want to stay immersed in the worst part.... But then, what is the real story? I don't want to stop writing."

"No, both your adult self and the little girls seem to want to continue," she said.

"I guess, when I stop trying to write the really ugly stuff, that I am writing about finding the little girls and their finding me. I need to tell how I learned to be trustworthy for them and they learned to trust me, and I learned to trust you, Sarah."

"It's a love story," she said, "a love story of you and the little girls."

The River

≈ 18 Dreaming Water

IT'S THE RIVER, ALWAYS. All my years from four to fifteen, the river that bordered our back yard was a given. The river and the tides it carried from Long Island Sound twice a day, the time of high tide advancing 52 minutes each day. The waters, the tang and slap, the gifts they gave me of lives to watch. The delicate shrimp rippling their legs. The mussels' mouths opening their careful quarter inch as the tide rose over their heads, showing the wavy, fragile lines of the lips inside.

The remembered smells of the river hang in the back of my nose, the salt heaviness utterly authoritative and basic, and the accents—low-tide stench or sharp brightness of the dried reeds—telling about seasons and weather.

In my dream, I am at the dock on the river, and the tide is nearly high. The reeds, mussels and seaweed sway in the waves to the right of the dock. Then the tide is out a bit, so the shore is just at the end of the dock. I am standing on the last part of the oyster-shell beach as the tide sinks towards the mucky part. Two people in a boat row by and they scatter some powder on the water, obscuring it. I am frustrated, knowing I won't be able to see down in to catch the crabs that swim in the deep water around the rocks next door.

In real life, the water was laden with sewage from all the pipes that went directly from the houses into the water, carrying pee, toilet paper, turds, and occasional condoms that I didn't understand until I got older. The Italian family next door ate crabs from the river all summer, but my mother decreed, because of the pollution, that we could catch and eat the crabs only once a year. Catching them took a string with bread on it, or anything at all edible, and the cotton string pulled up slowly hand over hand, until the last arm's length was done with just the left hand, the right arm holding the crabbing net with its gray galvanized wire hoop and knotted string net. The crabs swam up, graceful but wary, often darting away sideways just as the net approached. Because of the pollution, too, I was never allowed to swim there, although my father did.

In the dream, I am sculling a boat, standing up, with one oar, they way they do in China, the oar anchored to an upright in the boat, and making S-curves in the water. I know how to do this, though I grew up rowing with two long wooden oars and oarlocks, like everyone else. Our boat, Old Ironsides, had rust stains in the bottom from the bailing can, a tomato can that was an absolute necessity because of the way the boat took on water. I learned to row before I learned to bicycle.

Then I am swimming in that forbidden water, making the same S-shaped curves, my legs strongly and gracefully propelling me forward. I know how to do this. I swim confidently across the quarter-mile wide river. I come to a place two-thirds of the way across, where someone has written on the water in clear, flowing letters of gold but it's in a foreign script, like Cambodian or Arabic, so I can't read it. I can't read it yet.

On the real river, that's where the tide flats showed up, black and sticky, when the tide went out. The flats were seed beds for little oysters. Wooden working boats came up river at the right season each year and tipped oyster spawn into the water so the little oysters would attach and grow on the flats. A season later, they would use nets to dredge the young shellfish and take them out to the harbor to grow to maturity.

It's the river, always. Impersonal life coming and going beneath the surface, fanning the water with fins or swimmerets. The power of the tides brings in a saltier knowledge from the big body of water a half mile away. It is the place of refuge, the dock of cedar posts and weathered planks warm in the summer sun. I know how to navigate these waters, whether in a boat or swimming. I have the grace to go into the murky depths, crabs or no. I swim above the oyster beds, the place where the young ones grow up.

THIS WEEK, I'LL BE taking a break from writing to go up to Maine to a rented cottage by another salt river, estuary—gulls, crabs, mussels. Going toward what I love. Leaving behind the notebooks full of mucky drawings, bringing the knowledge nonetheless. I feel the pull of the salt life, the tidal call of moon and water. My nostrils widen to catch a molecule or two of that pheromone: desire, self-knowledge, enjoyment.

≈ 19 At the Water's Edge

I WAS AT A CONFERENCE on the West Coast when the river dream came to me, about two years after the initial revelation. Waking in the tangled sheets of the queen-sized motel bed, I grabbed my journal and wrote down a brief account of it, but the dream was so vivid that the details are clear even now.

The last of the yellow leaves were hanging onto bushes and trees in Sarah's back yard when I saw her again. I told her about the conference where I gave a workshop. "The conference was OK. I was sick, actually, and so my session was kind of a blur, but I think we did well anyway. But I had this amazing dream..."

I closed my eyes and immediately sank into a trance as I pulled up the dream from a deep place. "It's the edge of the river where I grew up. The tide is partway out. Two people in a rowboat put powder on the water so I can't go catch crabs if I want to. Why would someone do that? I am sculling the boat, just one oar. I can do this. Then I am swimming, myself, with that sculling motion of my legs. I know how to do this. Far, far out in the river. I am strong. Finally, I turn back. There is writing on the water that I can't read."

"I can see," I said slowly, "that people who put the powder on the water are stopping me from seeing what is in there, like Myra and Jack. They don't want me to remember."

"Yes, that makes sense."

"And I feel, I can *interpret* it, the water is the unconscious, where I need to go. But somehow I don't *get* the dream. It feels really important, but it's a mystery." I was still feeling heavy inside, slowed down, deep inside this mystery. Opposite me, Sarah was quiet.

"I don't understand. I am drawn to the water. It feels like my medium. But I still have no clue. It feels like *nothing*. All is on the surface, it's nothing. Trivial. No problem. Everything is fine—nothing here, nothing happening.... Can you help me? I feel lost."

"Can someone there help you?" asked Sarah. "Is the little girl anywhere around?"

I saw an image of myself at nine or ten standing in the water. It was a photo my father must have taken. A long-legged little girl with pigtails was looking at the life in the jar she was holding, water running down from it. "Oh, I do see this girl from the photo. She is at the water's edge, she is so vivid. Bright. Full of life. I see her so clearly there.... But I don't want to lose her brightness," I wailed, knowing I loved this girl's eagerness, curiosity, zest. "I don't want to lose that."

"You don't have to lose it," said Sarah.

"But if things happened to you," I said to that girl, "if there are dark things in your life, I want to know about them. When you're ready, when I'm ready. Slowly." I held the image of being with that little girl.

"Now the little girl and I are going to the edge of the water where the dream began. The tide is out, out past the pier. We look at the water where somebody sprinkled that powder so we can't catch crabs if we want to. Why would somebody want to do that, cover it up? We wonder.

"A fog just came up. A scary fog. It seems like everything is bright and OK, or it is fog and we never will see anything, it will never be clear. I am holding the little girl's hand tightly. It helps. It's all totally unclear but we have each other. Standing there at the edge of the water, not getting our feet wet yet."

I came back up to ordinary awareness very slowly. "I really don't want to analyze that dream and try to make sense of it."

"That's fine—it's an amazing dream and it will do its work without you putting words on it." Sarah's face looked soft and affectionate.

"Oh, good. It seems like I will find out over time."

"Your connection to the little girl was beautiful," Sarah said. "You are doing wonderful, deep work. I hope you know that. Sometimes when you're speaking from the trance, it's like poetry."

"Thanks, " I said shyly. "I do feel that this little girl is strong and wonderful and full of life. We don't yet want to go beyond the surface. But we will."

"It's time to end now, but we can come back to this, as many times as you want. It's a powerful dream."

I wrote Sarah her check and we confirmed our next appointment. I stood up and hugged her as usual at the end of the session.

"Now take it slow this evening," she said. "You have done a lot of work here."

Sarah's words, her support for the beauty and necessity of this way, help me to enter into this dream-space. To stand at the edge of the water, with faith. I do want... (this can only be said hesitantly)... in time, to swim these waters, dive beneath these surfaces. Slowly. Low in my belly, I feel the pain.

I am developing a nourishing slowness. I have long been rushed. Slowness is an antidote to the pressure, a balm for the wounds of knowledge-too-soon.

I need to be able to surrender in some way, not to have to be too much grown-up, not to have to be the one to keep separate. I need to trust someone besides myself, in a deep and childlike way.

"I wrote you a poem, but I feel kind of scared about it," I said to Sarah at our next session. The late-afternoon sun was streaming in the windows. "It feels pretty risky."

"OK, take a breath." She looked at me with the warmth of a half-smile.

Her quietness felt encouraging. "All right, here goes," and I spoke slowly into the space between us.

Poem to transference

Ghost,
magic in which I willingly believe.
Cradling in your huge embrace,
sky and earth together.
How can I call on you?
My imagination demands an earth mother,
you are a bird-woman.
It's OK.

Paradox raised to the nth power.
Irrational—in mathematics,
a number that cannot be created
by ordinary arithmetic—
add, subtract, multiply, divide,
but this is of a different order.

The force of our collaboration
sets the air to humming,
calms the bees,
allows the dragon flight.

Perfect imperfect witness,
mother that (n)ever was.
Contentment; I'm not worried.
Let the power tremble the air.
It's only magic.
Let it be.

"Oh, I really like it. It's wonderful, very expressive."

I took another breath, relaxed a bit.

"Why was it scary to read? Was it the part about calling me a bird woman?"

"Yes. I feel shy of naming how I see you. And also saying that I really want an earth mother and you're not that."

"Sure." She chuckled, "I know I'm not exactly the earth mother type. But it's OK to feel that way."

"And it's kind of a big step, being direct about this relationship. I mean, naming that I want to feel like you're my mother."

"Mmm-hmm. That is a step."

"It used to feel more personal, my feelings for you. But now, it feels bigger, maybe more spiritual, bigger than either of us. Really magical and I don't understand it."

"It is true that this work can be huge and magical, and mysterious. You know, I am an ordinary person, and yet when people work together this way, and invest belief in it, the work can be much larger than both of them."

Ah, something opened inside like petals. I was so glad to be met in this feeling. She understood that it went beyond the personal and psychological. "It feels safer, being part of something larger."

"Yes, it is reassuring. And I really liked how you wrote about the magic in the poem."

Oh, yummy approval.

THE RIVER DREAM MARKED a watershed. Its images have dozens of meanings, still unfolding. Just recently as I was talking about this dream, Sarah said, "I think that one meaning of the writing on the water could be that it is the language of recovery that you would learn over time. You learned to trust and understand nonverbal images, movements, things you could express in drawings and even in silence."

"Oh," I said with awe. "It certainly is a different language than normal, logical speaking."

"It allows a much larger understanding and integration."

And again, as I pondered the dream while writing this memoir, I felt the buoyancy of swimming in the river. It was an encouragement to allow myself to be buoyed by the waters of trust.

IT WASN'T ALL SWEETNESS and light from Sarah. One day, I was complaining about feeling unsupported by my colleagues at work. I said, "I feel like you are thinking that I could get better support from them if only I did it right. If only I asked in the right way or said the right thing."

A short silence. "Can you own that? Can you see that you're projecting that onto me?"

Ouch! Painful, but true. "Yes, I do see that I am putting those thoughts on you. You didn't say that, it's just what I'm afraid of." Transference in its plainest form, expecting her to do the exact thing my mother would do. She cut that cord with a sharp knife.

≈ 20 Alone in the Snow

FINDING FRIENDS SEEMED impossible. My journals were stuffed with accounts of dinners with different people. I tried hard to work things out with my dance friend Sally, but our needs collided. We set up a dinner time and I waited at the Asian noodle place—twenty minutes, a half hour, forty minutes. Sally dashed in, panting. "Oh, I'm so sorry, I didn't allow enough time." And the next time, "Oh, the traffic was too awful!"

"Sally, I can't keep doing it this way. When you are so late over and over, it just makes me angry. My life is really busy and this feels insulting."

"Well, I just see time differently. I can't be held to a schedule. You know, my spiritual practice.... Besides, my other friends don't have a problem with it," all in her earnest, nasal tone.

What I did get from my intense friendship with Sally was the permission to talk for long periods about trauma, dissociation, defenses—topics that a lot of people don't want to touch.

MY MOTHER WANTED ME to drive down on Christmas Eve, have Christmas with her alone, then spend the next day with my sisters, Suzie and Kathy, then have another Christmas with my son, who would be with his father on Christmas Day. I thought I'd go mad if I had to be with her compulsiveness for three different celebrations.

I decided to take a retreat by myself for two days, and then visit her for a few days after Christmas, when my son could be there. I could tell she wasn't happy about it, but I insisted, while feeling odd and selfish.

There was crusty snow by the road as I drove to Sarah's house in the country just before I started my retreat.

After we settled into our chairs, I asked, "You remember how you suggested that I visualize a safe place inside me?"

"Uh-huh."

"Well, I tried, and I just got foggy, scary places. And an intense fear of isolation. Did you have any idea how challenging that would be, when you suggested that?"

"Maybe you could let it be for now."

"Ah, that feels like a good idea."

"I see it brings up all the old feelings, how much you did not get protected when you were little and how much you needed it."

"Yeah, I really needed it."

"I know it's hard, but it's OK to feel that need now."

In that session, I again found myself sinking way into a fog. "This is not where I want to go, it's all fog. Do you think you can help?"

Sarah said, "Something will occur, you will find a way to go where you need to go today."

Nothing. Gray. Indistinct. Nothing. Everywhere. In all directions. I keep thinking I'll go somewhere. Nothing. Gray. Empty. No features no way, the same everywhere. I kept reporting back: "Nothing, empty. No hope. No way out."

"I'm sorry—we have to stop soon. How about if you tell the child that we'll make a time to come back," Sarah said.

"I will be back, little one. You won't be alone....

"But Sarah, I thought I would be feeling that sharp pain of loneliness, or else I would be holding and comforting the child. This is really confusing."

"I think maybe the child needs you to feel and really witness this bleakness just as she experienced it. I think that this is more important to her than the details of what happened. She may need you to fully *get this* before being ready to move on."

"Oh, that makes some kind of sense."

"It could be hard if the child wants you to spend more time in this bleak place while you're on retreat. I'll be there at the other end of the phone if you need to hear my voice or hear that you are doing OK." We made an appointment for the day after Christmas. *I like her telling me I can call. It makes the struggle real—she sees it and acknowledges it.*

After I drove home from therapy, I began my retreat on a cloudy, snowy afternoon. I cleared the kitchen table except for a little offering place with a fat red candle, a striped stone from the shore, and a small carved dragon, all inside the circle of mountain laurel root that I had found during my first retreat.

> *Empty out a space. This space is all mine. Some rules to keep clear and simple and inward:*
>
> *Yes to walking, writing, drawing, simple chores when I feel like it.*
>
> *No to reading (other than my own writing), phone calls, TV, people, puzzles, and activities.*

In the morning when I woke to a day of solitude, I felt lumpy, not special or dedicated. After a simple breakfast, I wrote in my journal at the kitchen table overlooking the backyard with snow accumulating on bare branches. I wondered whether I dared visit the gray, bleak place that I'd seen in therapy.

> *What a pushiness inside! Hurry, hurry, find insights. Impatience—will I ever move on?*
>
> *In order to move on, I have to be willing to stay here forever.*
>
> *I sit, I ask the little girl what she wants. I get nothing. I feel I'm not big enough, loving enough, to hold her and all her needs. I fear I'll never be big enough. I feel like my mother for a few moments. I feel her fear of not being able to take care of this child.*

Putting on my old-fashioned wooden snowshoes, I wandered for two hours in the woods in the deepening snow. There were no tracks ahead of me, neither from people nor animals, as the snow fell heavily. I felt isolated and without resources. All my lovely words about being discerning and creative and being able to follow my own thread felt distant—not worthless but not helpful either. Back home, I fixed a cup of tea and wrote more.

I don't know if I can find the thread. I feel lost. Maybe this is the experience of the little girl—the wasteland all around.

This is all dry, no water at all—not pain but despair: never going to have a hug, never going to hear someone say "I love you" and rejoice in that. Never going to feel simple warmth of sun. This place has no end and no boundaries, no people and no hope. A place with no shelter. I'm all alone, I'm so tired of this, this is totally boring as well as unpleasant and scary. I don't know how to get out of here.

It seems trivial. Doesn't everybody have this desolate place inside? There's no hope at all that sitting here solitary and brooding will get me closer to connection and people. I can't ever feel connected to the Lost Girl. She's lost out there but what use is it for me to sit and sulk and brood and be like her? I hear my mother and father in this condemnation.

The next day was Christmas. Before breakfast, I sat and invited Little Jane to draw whatever she wanted. First she drew in bright pastels, a funny squiggly creature with a girl's face. Then a dark, dark picture, scribbles of black and dark blue oil pastels, with a few red and yellow slashes, the picture dense on the entire page. Little Jane asked, "Is it good?"

"Yes," I said, "It is a treasure. It goes way beyond what Myra and Jack would have you do. They don't want to see the darkness. They don't know how to value your doing this. This is a special adventure and you are very brave to be doing it."

The time now seems luxurious. I can hang out with the little girls and celebrate them. Each time I look at the dark picture I am moved again—so much pain and darkness shown clearly.

Two years of working with this doesn't feel so long. Drawing is a way of creating my self. My heart feels open and ragged at the edges.

After breakfast, I called Myra. We talked for a half hour about the weather, my trip down the next day, the presents she had for the others. I felt my Good Girl self taking charge and responding as expected. Afterwards, I told her, "Thank you, Good Girl, for doing this for all of us."

With oil pastels I drew a grainy yet monotonous field—gray, brown and white like dirty snow. It was detailed but featureless. Nothing going anywhere. It changed in my sight—snow, frozen river, abstract, concrete. Solid but untrustworthy. Blurry, specific, bleak, and lonely. It gave me details about feelings beyond words.

> *This is the way it felt inside, so lonely. Pain had to be hidden. You had to look OK on the outside. No one believed a child could have such landscapes inside. No one wanted to believe or wanted to hear. They ran away from you and your need and your truth.*

In another gray landscape, small footprints grew closer—the Lost Girl coming home.

MYRA WAS EDGY because I had been away from her home on Christmas Day, so she kept me busy with tiny questions. "When did you say Will is coming? Shall we do the presents before or after lunch? Use the tablecloth or placemats?" Coming into her orbit after my quiet retreat felt like walking into a nest of bees. Then we had the pleasant hubbub of presents with Kathy and her husband, Suzie, and Will.

The next day, Myra had more things for me to do. I took off to go to the drug store, time out for me. I called Sarah from a pay phone in a parking lot, feeling desperate for contact. "It's so hard to act OK when I don't feel OK. It's like the old days!"

"I can hear that. Remember, you can come home early, even if it feels difficult. Remember to take care of yourself and take space."

I felt her support. No rescue. Support.

She said, "You're at a vulnerable point. It won't always be like this. You deserve special care. Remember not to do anything extra." It was very hard to take that part seriously. With my mother's abilities dwindling, I felt obligated to fix things for her, run errands, and do chores she could not do.

It was snowing again that evening when I asked my son to go for a walk with me. The streetlights made cones filled with drifting flakes. We walked in a comfortable silence for five minutes before

I drew breath to tell him, "I'm having a hard time being here with Myra."

"Uh," he said sympathetically, and looked down sideways at me.

"I... there's that early childhood stuff I'm dealing with that's really hard... it connects to her, the way she is."

He was quiet but I felt his listening.

"Can I have a hug?"

"For sure." He reached out to me and held me tightly while the snowflakes dissolved on my cheeks.

"Is it OK with you when I talk about family stuff? It's not disturbing?"

"It's always better to talk," he said, with the confidence of youth.

"I can't explain it to you now, but I will when I can. I'm just really vulnerable right now."

"It's OK, Mom."

≈ 21 The Flag Is Up

SEATED IN MY FAVORITE rocking chair with the curtains drawn against the freezing, starry night, I wrestled with words to capture the magical intensity of my dependence on Sarah.

> *How does it work that the surrender to this need for a good mommy allows it to be less painful? It doesn't make any sense. Growing up I learned how to put the need for love at a distance, so I wouldn't feel it so much. How is it that letting its knife edges cut deep to the bone can make it easier?*
>
> *This one person, whom I see only an hour or two a week, can't possibly take care of it all, can't possibly pay back the huge overdue debt of need that is inside me. No way. I go ahead, bit by bit, to do this illogical, irrational, risky! placing of my soul in her care, my heart in her hand—and it is a miracle how much better I feel. She says go ahead, it's all right to need me, while she sets boundaries too, keeps her hours (but welcomes those panicked phone calls generously). Somehow it works.*

Excited, I typed up my musings and printed them out. When I held the page in my hand, I felt an urge to send it to Sarah, whom I wouldn't see for nearly a week. I looked up her zip code and imagined her receiving it.

I put on my winter jacket to go to the mailbox. It was a brisk and cloudy day with only the remnants of snow caked on the ground. The empty maples across the road were dancing against the sky.

The letter felt charged with the electricity of my relationship to Sarah. Automatically, I pushed back that feeling. *No-no, you shouldn't feel that way, it's temporary, it's not a real relationship, it's unequal, she doesn't think about you all the time, it's childish, it's just transference, you'll have to give it up some time.*

I put the letter in the box, feeling the crackle of connection to my hand, and closed the mailbox door. Walking back up the drive, I looked back again to make sure I had put up the flag on the mailbox, and suddenly felt, *Why not admit that the letter I addressed to her had a glow about it? That I needed to check twice to make sure the mailbox flag was up?*

IT WAS SNOWING LIGHTLY when I next drove up the dirt road to Sarah's house. As I sat on the couch, I could see the flakes filtering down through the hemlocks close by.

"I loved the writing that you sent to me," she said.

"Oh, thanks. I felt a little shy about it."

"It's really clear and strong and describes your feelings well. I'm really glad you were able to write it."

Phew! I guess she's not overwhelmed by my feelings.

"I wonder... you remember that description you wrote me about sinking into an underwater trance state? I might want to use that—not with your name, of course!—in that presentation." Sarah had told me that she was giving a talk to a local professional group where they were studying hypnosis and trance. She had already asked about using my session about the river dream as an example, especially the interaction with the child.

"Oh, yes, I'd be pleased." I felt a belly-warmth knowing that she saw my work as valuable. "You know, when I went to send that writing to you, I felt such a charge in the letter, sending it to you. I really noticed how my inner voices tell me to pull back and not allow the love to spill over."

"Uh-huh?" Her brown eyes looked at me kindly.

I closed my eyes and let my breathing slow down, bringing up words from deep. "It feels like it's all about love and trust, connection. How scary it is to love someone. Does this make sense?"

"Oh yes, this makes complete sense. I hear you. It's important stuff."

"I know that I have been openhearted as a mother and with students, and I need to value that."

"Yes, that's true."

"But with others sometimes I feel like people just don't hear me, and I just don't know where to begin really connecting. I guess I need to work with this."

"We'll take it one step at a time."

Let this happen. I feel the resistance of "oh-no you can't possibly be so vulnerable, trite, excessive," but then I feel soft, permitted, tender, unguarded.

So long I have been careful and bounded. It's OK to love Sarah this much, this way.

The old unthinking fear. Fear that love, if I let it, would be an overwhelming, uncontrollable tsunami, drowning me and battering me beyond recognition.

≈ 22 Rocky Road

"I WANT TO GET together a therapy group for abuse survivors," Sarah told me one day in the winter of my isolation. It was at the end of our session and the light was fading outside. "This would be for people who are ready to work in depth, to use art or other creative media for exploration. Wouldn't it be good to have some companionship in this?"

"Yeah, I guess so. If it really would be the kind of place where I can do this deep work, where I can sink down inside."

"I hear a hesitation?"

"Well, I'm afraid of being different again, like in grade school where I was too far ahead of the other kids. I would love to be with other people doing the inner work. But would it be that way? Or would I feel lonely again?"

Six months later, in early summer, Sarah said she was going to go ahead with the group. "But it's going to be a little different. The people in there are not as far along as I hoped, but they are good women, and I think it will come along."

AT THAT SAME TIME, I felt a new stirring, the small, vague presence of a girl who wanted to be seen without words.

Feelings come first. I need to hear your feelings. Stories can come later, you don't have to bring me words. I can feel how you feel, I can see how you move, I can hear your sounds. That's plenty.

I can be clear without words. Sarah can be my witness without words. That would be a way. It feels liberating, a real idea.

I went to see Sarah on a June morning with the robins chirping loud outside the window.

"I think I need to go into some wordless place. Will you help me try it?"

"Of course. Why don't you settle in and just breathe."

Therapy without words? I felt doubtful even though I had proposed it. I spoke out loud to Little Jane, "It's OK, little one. I am so glad you are here, just here, no matter what you say or don't say."

Painful, twisted, and crying—the feelings came upon me. My mouth made whimperings. My hands and feet writhed and twisted. I really let go into it, flopping around on the sofa.

Sarah made softly sympathetic sounds opposite me, not interrupting or speaking.

After some ten or twenty minutes, I stopped *being* the little one. I held her in my arms, feeling the physical solidity of a small girl's body. "How brave you are to do this, little one."

I heard Sarah saying, "Yes, you were brave."

"Not everyone will do this. It's really brave and important for you to let us see how you feel. You don't have to use words." I sat a long time feeling the little one on my lap. I grew bigger, my shoulders expanding as she rested there. "Rest. You don't have to go further. Let it be, let go of the need to go further. You are fine right here."

I returned slowly, opened my eyes and looked at Sarah.

"That was important work," she said. "Very profound and painful. I was so moved to see the little girl's pain directly. As I witnessed, I needed to be careful not to be overwhelmed by the pain it evoked for me. I closed my eyes a bit and breathed."

"Oh, I could hear you breathing sometimes." It felt very intimate to have her say how it affected her.

"This kind of movement work is more familiar to you than to me," she said.

"I guess it's OK to do therapy this way. It feels right."

"Yes, it's more than OK. It's really good work."

As I drove back home I felt very tender that the little girl was showing herself in a wordless, incredibly vulnerable way. I remembered how I had taken time with the Lost Girl in the barren bleak place, stayed with her forever until it changed. *We will take that kind of time,* I thought. I suspected that not many people would stay in a wordless agony place and that people did not want to see it. *Sarah is strong. I'm not worried. She can see it well and still be OK herself.*

THE OFFICE IN THE CITY felt pretty small for the seven or eight assorted chairs circled for our first therapy group meeting. Calm, abstract watercolor paintings on the walls were lit by the evening sun. I was nervous watching women of various ages filtering in and seating themselves. Who were these other women who were also survivors? What would they be like? Would I find a safe place here? How would it be to have my therapist leading the group? Would I feel jealous when she turned her attention to others?

At the beginning Sarah introduced herself and talked a little about the purpose of the group. "We are not here to tell our full stories. We want to focus on how we are recovering, what is happening in our lives right now." She didn't talk about how it would be structured, and I was wondering.

Each woman introduced herself, and I was last. Some women went on and on, and I could feel my fear. *I won't have time. There's no limit on what others can do— that means I will be pushed aside.* I noticed that some of the people who talked a lot gave painful details, but in an emotionless way; that was confusing and frightening to me.

I don't feel safe here. What is the structure? There are so many people and so little time. I just know I won't be heard.

When it finally came around to me, I said, "I am feeling alone here and isolated. I just came from a three-day faculty workshop, so maybe that is why I feel so alienated. I am scared that no one will hear me. I don't know about this group. I'm twenty years older than all of you."

"No." Both Sarah and one of the women spoke at the same moment.

"I'm forty-eight, not that much younger than you," the woman said.

"I told you there would be a range of ages," Sarah said.

That didn't help much. I lashed out at Sarah in anger, "Why should I trust you?" I felt awful. There was a shocked quiet.

"Oh, God. I know I isolate myself and I mistrust people. It's really hard for me to talk here tonight." Then I told them that I'd begun to suspect the abuse three years earlier, after my father died.

Sarah explained to the group, "I want to work in depth with you, one by one, with the group as witnesses."

"But I want the conversation, the cross-talk, so I don't feel alone," one woman said. Others chimed in and the discussion went on with no decision about structure.

At the end of the session, as people were leaving, Sarah asked me if I was all right. "No, I'm not," I said.

"Stick around then, we can talk."

She spent fifteen minutes with me, trying to reassure me that this was just the beginning, that people needed time to get to know one another, that the group would develop.

> *Sarah's group—Ouch! ouch! My new little girl needs a lot less words and more direct feelings. I honor that. I hope Sarah can, too. I'm not running away from all contact, I just need a different medium that does not lend itself to such a barrage of words.*

The next time I had a session with Sarah, I arrived furious and scared. I said I needed to vent first.

"Fine, go ahead."

"There are no rules in the group, no clarity, no structure. It feels unsafe. People just go on and on. I'm so afraid there won't be space for me. What do I do about feeling overwhelmed by people talking around and not getting to things? I thought we were supposed to work in depth. It's unbearable."

"I hear you. I want the group to set its own ground rules, and we should do that next week. All the things you said are good questions that you can bring to the group."

"I really don't trust that's going to work. I want you to make some structure so I feel like at least I'll get some time."

"The group will work it out. That's the best way."

"Oh, man. I really don't see how that will work."

"You grew up as an only child. You didn't have the experience of working things through with siblings, so making your way in a group might be extra hard. And maybe this just isn't the time for a group for you."

"I think I do want to be in it, it feels intriguing, but it just can't be this hard."

"The group has to build trust over time. It will be chaotic at first. You need to take care of yourself in that setting, maybe space out or even sit back and do some drawing."

At the end of our session, she hugged me a long time, warmly, and said, "I'm here—you can call when you need to."

AT THE NEXT GROUP meeting, Sarah said we would have a little time for check-ins, a couple of minutes each without feedback, then we would set up some guidelines. She then asked Wendy a question to follow up from last week. Wendy answered, and Sarah then asked us all for responses.

"Wait," I said. "Where are we? You said two different things we were doing, but now it seems like we're doing something else again."

"Let's talk with Wendy first, then do brief check-ins, and get to the guidelines." We didn't get to any guidelines that night. People didn't check in for just a few minutes—several went on and on, and Sarah and the group responded.

One woman, Robin, had multiple personalities. This evening something set her off, and an angry little-boy character came out yelling, demanding all the attention in the room. Sarah asked Robin to sit on the floor by her chair. She stroked Robin's head and shoulders to comfort and calm her. I felt wildly jealous and intrigued. *Can I get that kind of attention? How come Robin gets to have all that contact?*

I asked Sarah for an extra individual session to talk more about my difficulties in group. "I feel insecure not knowing how it will go." I said. "I don't think I'm asking for rigid structure, but I want to know that I'm going to get time and attention."

"Groups deepen over time. You can't expect it to start out that way. People need time to get to know one another and learn to feel safe." It felt like she talked on this topic for a long time.

Who was this woman who was lecturing me about how I should feel? She didn't seem like my dear Sarah at all. She was telling me I should be patient, should be quiet, should think of others. She sounded just like Myra! When I protested, she tried harder to convince me rationally. Where was the nurturing Sarah who listened to irrational, scared little girls? I was terrified and furious, scared of losing everything with her.

"Wait, let me check in inside and see how I'm feeling. We don't have much more time, so I want to be clear." I sat feeling the press of tears inside my eyes, the frustration in the downturn of my mouth.

"I think it's too many roles. If I come to you with problems about the group, am I coming to the group leader or to my therapist? I feel like you've been responding as the group leader. Where's my therapist?"

She seemed frustrated, "You've been snapping at me a lot."

I slowed down. "I don't want to snap at you, I want to go into the issues that make me want to snap at you."

Then I sighed and tried to get clearer. "I feel like you are coming at me with words. They are such reasonable words. It makes me feel really little and like someone big is telling me the way I ought to be. It's happened too much before. Please don't lecture me!"

> *Is no one else like this? I get nauseated, I get overwhelmed. I feel like I have no power and I am going to be trapped and forced—all these explaining words coming at me, telling me why I am wrong, I should see it their way. Where is my voice in all this?*

BACK AND FORTH I went, week by week. It was interesting to see others, like me, trapped in family situations that felt unhealthy, unresolved, and binding. Some women had to tell long circumstantial stories about relationships and what everyone said to them. I hesitated to bring my little girls and their foggy, shadowy places into this mix.

A few times Sarah worked intensively with one person, the rest of us witnessing. Then I loved watching her interact, seeing how she listened and adapted to where the person was, finding the core feelings. That felt real and emotional. When I had a chance to get that kind of attention, I talked about how long I'd been a Good Girl and done what other people wanted, how much I needed attention for the little ones who were hurt and scared.

Robin and her multiple selves were fascinating to me. And maddening, when her alternate personalities burst into the room and took up all the space. On the day when I talked about the little girls inside of me, she came up to me as the group was breaking up.

"I was so relieved that you talked about little girls!" she said. "Nobody else is talking about kids inside and I really was wondering what's up with these women."

We walked outside the building and stood talking before we went to our cars. I felt touched and warmed to be connecting with her.

I liked Robin but I was scared of her, too, because she was so volatile. People stepped gingerly around her, afraid to set her off. One evening Robin said to the group, "Some of us have really deep wounds, and other people, like you," (looking at me) "have paper cuts."

"Paper cuts! Wait a second, you don't know about me. We haven't told our stories. You don't know my background."

Robin's body slumped and her face crumpled into tears. She started talking like a little boy, lashing out at me. With Sarah's help she managed to contain it fairly soon, but I felt I had unleashed chaos, and I wasn't sure that my words had been heard.

I MET WITH SARAH in her home office on a hot but breezy July afternoon. I said, "I felt better about the group last week, with the work that people did."

"I'm glad to hear that."

"But I still need to talk to you about coming at me with words, like when you tell me over and over that I need to wait and let the group develop."

"I thought you wanted explanations. I thought it would be reassuring to tell you how groups develop and how it might go over time. It always takes time to develop trust. And people are at different places." And she kept talking in the same vein.

"Oh! I'm so frustrated! It feels like you are talking at me again."

"I feel like I can't say anything, nothing I say will be right."

I took a very deep breath and tried to find a calm place inside that knew what was happening. "You talked about thinking I wanted explanations. How about instead saying something positive? Instead of justifying yourself, something like, 'I want to hear your feelings. You don't have to be reasonable or grown-up. I really want to work this through with you.'"

She said each of these things back to me, slowly.

I breathed, an exhale of relief.

"I do admit I've been feeling defensive," she said. "You seemed so critical of the way I was running the group, how it looks disorganized. I was afraid, if you stayed in the group I'd be constantly worried about you criticizing me. I felt I really had to show I am a professional."

I guess I hit a few buttons there! Wow! "I kind of sensed I wasn't the only one with feelings here. Thank you for telling me what is going on in you. I kept feeling something and it helps to know what it is." I sat quiet for a few minutes, sensing my reactions to what had happened. "I think I'm clear now, I think it's OK."

> *When the clash feels so irresolvable, we are both operating from hurt places. Acknowledge that.*

> *The delicate line of separation and roles. She's been awfully good at keeping her own troubles, when they happen, out of my line of sight. Here, I could see some real rawness. I see how my challenging her was fierce. I came on strong, so she defended herself. Not what you want your therapist to do, but it's human. Sarah doesn't have to be perfect.*

The group was far from being a place in which people dropped in deeply or did art work. We were clawing at the basics. After several weeks, we still had not talked about guidelines. I did not know how to handle the chaos.

> *Transference misery. I just hate the way that sharing Sarah takes away some of the magic. I need that magical quality. Yes, it's not rational, it's not grown-up and all of that. It's just there—feeling wounded and abandoned, feeling I want a really special connection and not getting it. I fear I'm supposed to be reasonable and good. I wail and wail.*

Finally, I got clear that it just wasn't working for me to be in the group and also be in individual therapy. In her warm office in late August, I said to Sarah, "The little girl wants to talk first, so the grownups won't take over and bicker."

"All right," she said, and I thought she looked wary.

Little Jane spoke through me. "I can't be there in the group much. It's too confusing and I really have a hard time finding space for me. And here in therapy it's hard. The grownups are always talking. Sarah talks with Big Jane and I have to interrupt to get heard. I don't like it."

"I hear you. You really deserve space."

"I was just starting to come out in June, when I asked you to see me without words, then Blam! the group. It's too hard. And all those different roles—grownup, child, group member, all talking to your different roles—too complicated."

"I heard the little one loud and clear."

I paused. "Are you disappointed in me?"

"No, not at all. There's too much of a gap between where you are and where the others in the group are. I had to try it in order to see."

WHEN I RESOLVED to leave after seven group sessions, I felt frantic. My trust in Sarah was slipping away in the group and in the arguing around it. I was paying for extra sessions in which to wrangle and come to no conclusion.

Finally, I had to let all the grown-up part go, stop arguing about how the group *might* go, stop offering criticisms, and just insist on getting care for the little one. Years later, as I wrote this chapter, my mistrust came back with gale force and I needed to talk it all through with Sarah again. It still felt lumpy, as she defended her view that the group would have evolved, but then conceded, "I wouldn't run a group like that again. The needs were just too diverse."

And I said, "I know it wasn't a good time for me to start being in a group, with the wordless little one just making herself known. I know how withdrawn and scared I was. I'm not sure I could have been in any group just then."

"That was a hard thing. The group would have taken time to evolve. Just the way you don't get close to a new friend all at once."

"Well, if I had a new acquaintance like that group, I wouldn't keep on seeing her and trying!"

"Yes, it was good you got out. And as it was, I ended the group a month or so later—it just wasn't working."

"It was pretty trying for our relationship. It scared me a lot."

"Maybe I didn't realize how scary it was to you in that way."

Moving On

≈ 23 To the Studio

"Hi, you're here!" My heart was beating fast as I opened the studio door. Sarah was fifteen minutes late, and I had wondered if she was coming.

"I'm sorry. I lost your directions and thought I knew where it was." Sarah took off her shoes and entered.

"Well, you're here. This is the studio where I've been dancing with my friend Pam. Don't you love the tall windows?"

"The big trees in the yard there and the view of the hills, I like that. It's a welcoming space."

"And the floor is like satin."

"Where do you want me to sit?"

I hadn't thought of that. "How about here by the door, even though I'll lock it. That could help me feel safe."

All summer, through the difficult passage of the therapy group, I had had fleeting thoughts of inviting Sarah to the studio to watch me move. The little girl who was so wordless wanted some way to be seen and understood, and sometimes sitting and talking was frustrating—especially that summer, of course, because of our long fight about the group.

Within a week after I left the group, I asked Sarah, "Would you come to the studio and watch me move? I mean, I know you're not a movement therapist, but you have done art therapy work, haven't you? My little one who doesn't want to talk, it seems like she could be there and you could see her."

"I'd like to see her. Let me think about it a bit."

At our next session she said yes. I arranged for the studio and I called one of my movement teachers, Peter, who also conducted private movement therapy sessions.

"Can this work? I trust her a lot, but I'd have to really structure it myself, because she hasn't done this before, witnessing movement."

"You have a lot of experience and wisdom—I think you could hold that."

"Tell me how movement therapy is different from the work we do in groups, would you?"

"Sure. There's more focus on the individual. And then we work the transference explicitly." Mmm, that sounded a little scary, but I thought, *Well, maybe I don't have to do that.*

"I feel like the watching will be different," I said. "In Authentic Movement, my witnesses don't have to know what my issues are. I'm sort of protected. I think with my therapist watching, I'd feel really exposed and maybe shy because my movement would be showing so much."

"Yes, for sure it's different because the therapist knows so much of your history."

"I'm not sure how it would work, since I know the form and she doesn't."

"Well, I guess it's true you'd have to introduce her to that, and that puts you in a slightly different position, but it sounds like you have a good working relationship with Sarah..."

"Oh, yes."

"...and if she has the flexibility, I think you can do fine with it. Congratulations! It's really exciting that Sarah is willing to do this—not every therapist would be so flexible and willing to try. Let me know how it goes, if you want. I have every confidence in you."

Sarah had brought a back-jack to sit on, and she placed it on the floor and sat down. I had brought my favorite pillow. I locked the door and we began.

"Maybe I should warm up a few minutes and you can just watch."

"That's fine."

I stretched, bending over and touching my hands to the floor, finding tight places in my sides and neck. I did some rolling on the floor, somewhat self-conscious about being watched in my habitual moves by a new person. Then I returned to a place near Sarah and decided what to do next.

"Maybe I could just move whatever comes and you could watch. Would you let me know at twenty minutes?" It felt important to have some kind of boundary.

At first I rolled on the floor, having fun with my body. Then it turned serious. I could feel something in my mouth and I wanted to hide, cheek against arm, hide my face. No one should see my face, I felt so ashamed. *Help, I'm going....*

I stopped and slithered across the sweet floor to a spot about two feet away from Sarah. I squirmed and inched closer, about a foot away, and put my head on my pillow. My heart pounding, I asked, "Would you put your hand on my head?"

"Sure." She did, her fingers in my hair.

"And tell me it's OK?"

"It's OK. It really is OK." Her fingers stroked tentatively through my hair.

I cried and whimpered, it felt so good. "I need so much to stay with this and not have to explain or put words on it."

"That's fine. Just stay here."

I stayed for several more minutes, basking in her caring touch. Then I sat up. "What do you think? I feel it's working."

"I'm very comfortable in the watching and not talking much. It feels fine. I am really excited that you are doing this, and so pleased—honored, really—that you asked me to come here."

"This feels so new. Scary and exciting."

"Do you want to meet in the studio at our regular time on Tuesday?"

"Oh, I'd really like that." *I want to see you next Thursday, too.* I didn't say right then, but later I asked to see her twice a week in the studio.

As she was picking up her things to leave, Sarah said, "I love this studio. It makes me want to dance."

I got confused—did I want to see her move? I was so used to the reciprocal process in authentic movement and it was tempting to want to see her as another human being. "Do you want to warm up together at first?"

"No, I don't want to take up your space."

Relief and disappointment. The time was for me. It was not that kind of relationship. What was our relationship in the studio?

Different witness, different context, different intent. She's my therapist, she knows so much. I bring the same inwardness as in authentic movement, the idiosyncrasy, individual gestures, young places. And because it's therapy, I am offering all of myself, no hiding.

She doesn't know the conventions of authentic movement. We're making it up as we go.

It's not reciprocal. It's a place for the child to get to be fully herself, not care-taker or grownup. Asking Sarah to comfort me, stroke my head, that's very much the needy child.

My need for this feels immense and wonderful. About a year and a half of just being held and comforted, that might be about right, nothing else.

LABOR DAY ARRIVED again and I went to stay with Myra, while I practiced taking care of myself. I went to the bookstore and got a cup of coffee before running the errands at Home Depot and fixing things at her house. I told Good Girl that she was terrific and deserved the breaks.

At supper as we watched the TV news, Myra said vehemently, "What are they doing bombing one another in Europe? How can they do that?" and "How can the Russians trust Yeltsin? I never would. Why?"

I wondered whether she was expressing her own despair, anger, and helplessness projected onto the world as metaphor. "Tell me, why are they doing it?" she demanded of me. Both in her political rants and in her endless need for me to do chores for her, she kept asking for something that couldn't be given because she couldn't receive it.

THAT FALL I WAS RELEASED from work into a blessed semester of sabbatical, which I decided to dedicate mostly to personal growth.

> *I need to go to disgusting crazy yucky weird places I can't explain. Can I trust Sarah to hold it and not have to have words or have it make sense? I need to do it and I don't want to be alone.*

When we met in the studio, I didn't have many words. I established a little ritual to make safety. Talk a bit. Sit silently for a minute. Warm up in the space for five or ten minutes. Return to Sarah and be touched and comforted. Move for twenty minutes. Do a drawing while she watched me. Sit and talk about it all. Ask her to hold me, feel the comfort of her.

This time, after the initial parts, I asked, "Will you tell me when it's twenty minutes?"

"Of course."

I crawled out into the space and then curled on my side. I covered my head with my hands and rocked a little, then writhed slowly. Every part of me was confused. Nothing made any sense. I kept moving, my hands first covering my mouth, then making swimming motions on the floor. My stomach was gripped with nausea, my ears were buzzing. The whole world was spinning unevenly and I couldn't feel which way was down. Inside my head, colors of purple and yellow-green and gray, mixing and churning. I stayed with those feelings, and nothing got better.

"It's time now, twenty minutes."

I crawled back to Sarah and then sat close to her. "Oh, my god, nothing makes any sense. I just feel this overwhelming confusion where nothing in the whole world makes sense."

"Yes."

"I guess it's the little girl's world turned upside down, the huge betrayal, no one to trust, but having to trust her parents anyway."

"So confusing and awful."

"And I was not big enough to understand these strange things happening to my body."

"Yes, you were far too young to have these body-feelings."

"Does that mean I'm bad?"

"Oh, no. No, I don't mean your little one is bad. He was bad for making this happen, making you have the feelings. I just mean that you were too little to have these grown-up feelings forced on you. That was wrong."

"Oh. Not my fault?"

"Not your fault."

"Can I put my head in your lap?"

"Yes, that's fine. Here's the Kleenex."

I wept and wept. Even my confusion could not be expressed back then when I was little—all of it bottled up inside, all this time. I wept and felt very small. Small and cared-for, small and held.

It was powerful and very direct, being in that young confused and not-understanding place. Asking for comfort and receiving it. At the same time I had created this space: rented the studio, requested this structure, asked for this comfort. And yet Sarah's generous care flowed beyond the boundaries, embraced me in unexpected ways, as when she reached to touch my hand, watched me draw, and said she would hold me, if I wanted.

> *"Magic with everyday objects." Watch the matchbox turn into a studio with dancing women in veils. Sarah is a goddess with a bad back. A timeless presence who shows up late.*

MY WOMEN'S GROUP met in a red upholstered booth at a Chinese restaurant, celebrating someone's birthday. The talk alternated between politics and trivial things. In the months since I'd told them about my mouth memories, the group had drifted back toward a more superficial level. I had negotiated with them to try a different structure with more opportunity to talk in depth, but nothing much had changed. That evening I was patient and went along with the flow.

Driving home, I could feel Little Jane's distress. She felt a keen need for care and love. She couldn't bear to be around people who were chatting and chattering.

> *This is too hard, too painful. I can't do this. Two sessions per week just barely scratch the surface. I feel like I need a colony where everyone knows but I don't have to talk about it. An island where it's OK to cry and wail out loud.*

As I sat with the little girl the next morning, I felt a calm pool in my stomach after the tears. It was finally clear that my needs were still at cross-purposes to everyone else. I had to leave.

That morning I felt in my guts a yearning for beauty. I went to a nearby reservoir and danced barefoot on the pine needles. How desperately Little Jane needed to be listened to, needed to do just what she wanted.

> *Listen to her desires! Wow. My mouth feels full with other people's desires. Empty out and listen to the child's. Following my own desires did make me feel less teary and desperate.*

Believe it or not
it's right here
the clouds are dancing
the trees are dancing
my heart is dancing
its little every-second choreography
right here where I am
not on some Himalayan peak
not someone else's idea of what I need—
chatter, company.
This place
the common beauty of life
a big woodpecker hole
in that pine tree
insects in the last great exhale of fall
sun pumping life into all of it.

≈ 24 A Dock

It takes a while to enter fully into movement today, but now—past the shyness around Sarah, the fear of judgment and interpretation—I'm in deeper. Spiraling.

Mouth sickeningly full, nausea rising. Slow. Not-knowing. Knowing. So small I am. I must follow this turn, this hurt, this curve, the need. I must follow and follow. I am slowly turning on the floor, hand after foot, my body pulled into a heap, one hand covering my mouth. I see a spiral with my mouth at the center.

"It's been twenty minutes," Sarah said softly into the air of the studio.

I stopped and crawled to a place close to her, pulling my sketchbook and pastels towards me. While she watched, I drew the image that had come during moving. At the center, a black hole of a mouth, the shadows of two eyes above, two black outlines of hands trying to block the face, fingers spread to fend off. Through it all, a spiral of purple, circling dizzily inward to the mouth.

"The mouth. That's so hard for me to be with. Him doing that to my mouth, it stops me from speaking, breathing. It's the worst."

"Yes."

"Would you hold me a little while?" She did, in a sitting hug. I liked the feel of her nubbly cotton sweater on my face, and how her shoulder felt solid. I could take in some of the comforting.

I went back out on the floor. Soon I was lying on my back, experiencing a strong image of being under water. I saw the ripples of the surface above me. My fingertips traced the surface. I was inside the river dream and breathing underwater. Everything slowed down.

It doesn't have to make any sense. Follow, follow, trust. Nothing has to happen.

The river dream could be a map for where I'm going. I desperately want a map. The dream— the bank, the shore and the edge. Here I am now, swimming in it. I know how to do this. Yet to come: reaching the middle, deciding to go back. Seeing the writing on the water.

Sarah is here. She is strong enough to hold it all. I don't have to explain it to her or to anyone. It's all right that it is chaotic.

"You're still here," I said as I crawled back. It felt like a miracle. She didn't go away, the way my mother did. She was still there and witnessing, willing to see and hear my pain and confusion. For a while I lay on my back, snuggled up against her legs.

As we hugged goodbye that afternoon, Sarah said, "It's really a privilege to be here for such deep work with such integrity. It's beautiful. I was telling my colleagues in my peer group about this, really pleased with how it's going."

I loved hearing that my work was beautiful—an antidote to the ugliness and shame that it evoked.

The next time we met in the studio, I moved for a few minutes, curled around my pain, then asked, "Will you come sit next to me and touch me?"

"Sure." She moved close to me and touched my back.

"No, not there, please."

"Is touching on your neck OK?"

"I think so, try that.

"Mmm." A minute later. "Now stop, please."

"OK."

"Now more." So amazing! It started to feel legitimate to say, "Please touch me," and then, "Stop, not there."

I sat up to talk. "Thinking about touch, I've been remembering something my father said to me when I was an adult." Sarah listened with interest.

"When my son was about seven, we were at my parents' house for Christmas. Will and I were horsing around on the couch by the picture window in the living room, tumbling off the couch onto the carpet, play-wrestling and just being in contact for fun.

"Jack was sitting over by the fireplace watching us. He said, 'It's really odd to see you doing that.'

"I asked him, 'Why?'

"He said, 'I stopped touching you when you were five. It was to keep you from getting Electra complexes.'

"I said, 'What?' I felt like I'd been thrown onto my back on the floor.

"He said, 'You know, the Freudian theories. I didn't want you getting any ideas.'"

"That's pretty stunning," Sarah said.

"Yeah. That was long before this stuff about the abuse came up for me. But it just felt so weird to hear a man say that he was afraid his daughter would fall in love with him, that the *daughter* would be perverted. It was so backward, but I couldn't see it clearly."

"What else did you feel?"

"I felt that was so sad, to take away the pleasure of touch from a child, not to hold her safely in a hug, not to horse around with her."

"You're right, loving and safe touch is vital to a child."

"Later, I got angry. It really pissed me off that he assigned the sexual feelings to the girl, claiming that she could have an Electra complex. I hadn't identified the abuse but I knew it was really wrong to blame a five-year-old for sexuality."

"For sure! That is putting it in the wrong place. Did you stop horsing around with Will?"

"Absolutely not! I kept on."

"Good. You didn't let your father mess up your relationship with Will."

"I FEEL LONELY a lot," I said to Sarah one day. "Do I have to be alone?"

"I'm here. I'll be here as much as another human being can, within my limitations. I will come as close as you want. I can't be inside your memories and I didn't experience it as you did, but I'll be here."

Relief—she's not going away. Poignancy—she can't be in my memories; there is always a distance. And solidity—she's honest about the way it is, not pretending she can get inside and fix it or even be with it the way I am.

"You won't run away?"

"I won't run away."

"It's OK to go slow?"

"It's just fine to go slow. Go in little-girl time."

I sighed and lay on the floor next to Sarah, my eyes closed, feeling young. It was delicious to be able to ask the hard, easy, dumb questions. Like "Will you run away?"

After a while I sat up and asked, "But what about other people to be with? It's really hard to share this stuff—it's so young and vulnerable. But if I don't share anything, I feel all alone."

"Who are you thinking of?"

"Well there's Helen, she really is capable of hearing things in more depth, but it doesn't always happen that way. Pam is so passionate and I know she's on my side, but then she'll go off on some rant..."

Sarah said, "Take it slow. Remember that your relationship with yourself, with your little girl, is the most important one there is."

As I delved deeper into the wordless work in the studio, my tolerance for social chat nose-dived. Still, I tried to make friends. One promising relationship was with Helen, a woman I'd known slightly for several years. She was a quiet woman who shared my love of nature, and as we took long walks in the woods, I found I could share details of my inner life with her. She understood the ideas about the inner child, and in time I was able to talk about "my little girls" to her without shyness.

Even with Helen, there would be times when she filled the air with mundane details as we were taking a hike. First I cancelled a couple of times we were to go out, then I needed to tackle it more directly. We were walking along a road near a reservoir, the fall air crisp in our faces.

"Helen, I need to say something."

"Oh?" she said cautiously and I could see her body stiffen.

"It's about the therapy work I'm doing now. I've told you how I need to work without words, when I go to the studio with Sarah."

"Yeah?"

"I think I need more silence with you, sometimes. Like when we are walking. Maybe I could tell you when I'd like to have some quiet?"

"Oh, am I talking too much?"

"Well… I wouldn't put it that way, but I have this enormous need for silence and not chat."

"OK, well, you let me know. I think that's all right."

That's a relief! It wasn't easy, but I could feel that Little Jane was very glad I'd spoken up and made more space for her.

The next time I hiked with Helen, I interrupted after the first fifteen minutes of chat, saying, "Can we go quiet now?"

"Oh, sure." So we walked in blessed silence for a half hour, only speaking if there was a bird or some other natural object to be noticed and appreciated.

> *Trust—if it's hard to believe in the little girl and all the yucky stuff that happened, it's even more amazing to believe in other people. Trust, that's a new frontier.*

My dance-friend Sally was being her usual self, wonderful in the studio but difficult in conversation. She still showed up late and took most of the air space. Then she moved out of town.

Pam was the woman who'd stood up for that little girl at the park; I loved her feisty energy. We had a weekly date to dance together on Sunday, except she often called to say she was too busy. Our studio time was great—always evolving, risky in the ways that art is. But she needed to talk urgently, long, and without interruption about each new conflict at work and with her family. If I wanted air-time, she might listen well, but more often she interrupted with her needs. Later I challenged her on that and our relationship went up in flames.

I tried out other friendships, but a lot of people did not want the kinds of intense conversation that I craved. Reasonably enough, they wanted to talk about books and politics. That was all right with me as long as we spent time on more self-reflective things as well, but my balance of desires at that time differed from most people's.

SARAH WAS SITTING on the floor in the studio with her back against the wall. It was a soft rainy fall day.

"I brought you some drawings," I said.

"Oh, good. I love your drawings. They are really expressive."

"I'm a little shy about this one. There's the blue water all around, like in the river dream, and here's this little girl in the water holding onto a yellow something—it just looks like a blob but it's a dock—or else it's you."

"Oh, I like it. I like seeing that the little one has something to hold onto."

"But this blob doesn't have any features. I mean, if it's you, it's not you as a *person*, just kind of a thing to hold onto. Is that OK?"

"Don't worry about it. Don't ever worry about it."

That touched me deeply, Sarah's reassurance that it was all right to depend on her as a faceless, primal object. "Don't ever worry about it" gave me permission to see her as what I needed, to project onto her the qualities of strength, dependability, love, and caring.

I told Sarah how thankful I was for the work of the past month. "I am working on this night and day, spending a lot of my sabbatical time on this work. What do other people do? Not everybody has the time."

"True. A lot of people don't have the resources—financial or personal, to work in the depth you do. And people make different choices."

"I think a lot of people—I remember the therapy group—a lot of people don't want to spend time down deep inside."

"Different people need different things."

"You know, I think even our fighting about the group did help. I mean, I got stronger by being angry with you."

"Mmm."

"And I think it helped a lot when you said you knew you weren't perfect. Somehow I think it helped with trust."

After therapy that day I went off to work at the college. At home that evening, the magic was gone. Little Jane felt lost and alone. I sat and held this crying child. Why wasn't trust a normal thing to me?

I suspect Sarah doesn't really care. I suspect she thinks I should be moving on. I know whose suspicions these are (Thanks, Myra!), but it still hurts.

My expectations of the world grow from the flesh of my parents' flesh— the betrayer and the collaborator. Now Little Jane needs so much the magic of a place where she can be watched lovingly with no briskness, no impatience.

Little one, this is important. Please believe me, you are worth it! Your soul deserves this. You have reached a place of beauty. Why would you want to move on? To stay here is an act of defiance.

"It felt so awful not trusting you," I said to Sarah when I saw her. "I seem to need to re-find connection over and over."

"Yes, that's the way it goes with learning new patterns."

"Oh." I paused, feeling shy and young. "Are you here?"

"Yes."

"I really can ask you again and again?"

"Yes, of course the little one needs to do that. Think how long she learned not to trust."

"Does everybody grow up like this?"

"No, some people do grow up with a feeling of trust. The parents aren't perfect, but good enough, so that the child learns that the little gaps are OK."

"I guess I have to learn that now. Sometimes I think that the feeling of betrayal is worse than what he actually did to me."

"Indeed, true, not having anyone to trust."

I lay on my back and pressed my shoulder and arm against her legs. Then I moved out into the space and felt the connection while separate. I hummed to myself and held my arms in a circle, feeling a swelling, buoyant sensation in my chest, knowing that Sarah's love was right there inside me. Then I asked Sarah to come and sit by me. Just to know I could ask.

I pressed myself against Sarah then moved away onto the floor, a delicious, scary back and forth.

Sarah said, "Yes, it's like a two-year-old, remember how they need to go out into a playground, then rush back to Mommy?"

It was work. It felt like magic, but it required continued acts of faith and commitment. I had to see and cope with the fact that Sarah was human—she was late, sometimes her attention lapsed,

Mystery

Temple of inmost things
where the unspoken,
the unspeakable, and
the ineffable
are all held
in the arms of the goddess.
Temple of mysteries
where the furies dance
flames swirling in twilight.

Place so sacred none but
initiates may enter.
Where I lay myself curled
on the altar of trust.
Where the ancient waters run
into a pool of all-healing love.
I thirst to write your holy mysteries.
I vow to protect your secrecy.

This is what I know of holiness—
giving over all the awful knowledge
contained in the body.
Holding and being held
no barriers.
Love flows from the Goddess,
through one mortal body
to another. This is what I know
of love. Acceptance of ugly
deeds held in gut and soul,
released into touch, mystery
not of forgiving but of
living beyond.

sometimes she misunderstood. At the same time, I cultivated the sense of magic.

After therapy, I took a hike up in the hills. The sunset was coming on behind the bare trees.

> *I feel I've been shot full of some amazing drug, my whole system blissed-out.*
>
> *Little One, I love the way that you said you were testing, not quite trusting. I loved the way you were willing time and again to snuggle and ask to be held, ask for reassurance. To be very little and show your need—that is Very Big, that is huge. Being such a fragile, needy little girl is a huge, huge step for us.*

Sacred—that's the word. I feel this was sacred work. The child was starting to show her true strength as the light inside me. She was reaching out for love and trust.

Sacred was my willingness to let Sarah walk into my soul, opening to the unguarded exposure. Sacred was her acceptance of all of me—needy, mistrusting, angry, confused—her willingness to be with it all. Sacred was our agreement to work beyond words, beyond clarity about what happened, and beyond definitions of what we were doing—the willingness to go into the vast unknown of body-memory and the unconscious. Sacred was the quality of energy and attention we both brought to the work.

The sacred is ineffable. Beyond words. Beyond the mind's logical grasp.

The sacred means connection—between people, between us humans and the universe. The sacred connects us to a greater Love.

≈ 25 A Bolt of Darkness

ALTHOUGH I WAS on sabbatical, I went in to work to check my mail, trudging upstairs to the faculty mailboxes. The boxes were open cubicles sitting in the hallway, and Roberta the secretary was stuffing them with that day's batch.

"Watch out," she said. "There's something really weird in your box," and she looked at me with curiosity and perhaps some sympathy.

I took out a fistful of mail and there in the second layer was a glossy postcard of the kind I avoided in souvenir shops in New Orleans. A cartoonish naked woman was sticking her impossibly long tongue out and arching her breasts up. On the other side, a scrawled message said, "I know how you got where you are, you slut." Black ballpoint pen, postmark Atlanta.

"Jeez!" I said to Roberta. "What is this about?"

"Damned if I know. Some nut case."

I was shaken but I thought, Well, nothing to do about it. No way to know who that nut is.

The story really had begun about two years before that October day, when a female colleague and I obtained a grant to run a conference and publish a book about college teaching.

The conference was terrific, with smart faculty from all over the country coming together to talk about teaching. (It was the meeting that came just before my Big Ugly memory.) Those who attended also contributed essays for the volume. Being good citizens, we included a list of contributors' addresses in the book so that interested educators could get in touch with the authors of these essays about teaching. As it turned out, this list made us vulnerable.

I tried to forget about the postcard until three days later, when I got another one with a different postmark, a different lewd woman, and the message "I hope you enjoyed it when you licked your pastor's 'love log.' Better than your research, you bitch." This one was postmarked St. Louis. Now my heart was going 200. I checked in with Roberta. "Yeah, the creep. He seems to have it in for you. I am really sorry."

A week later, I received a hand-addressed envelope with no return address. Inside was a Xeroxed hand-written document in the form of a "survey for women scientists."

"How many men did you have to sleep with to get your present position?" it began.

"How many actually qualified candidates were there when you got your job?"

At the end of the form were my name and address and a request to send responses to my address. An enclosed hand-printed note said that this survey had been sent to dozens of my scientific colleagues. Then I got a phone call from a colleague in Portland, Oregon. He said he'd received this so-called survey and wondered who was pulling a prank on me.

A woman at the University of Vermont called to tell me that she was extremely upset to get this "survey" and asked me what I was going to do about it.

"I don't know," I said. "How can I do anything? I have no idea where this is coming from." It was upsetting that she expected me to fix the problem.

I took the letter down to my colleague Lisa's office and told her. "Wow, that's awful. Terrible. You'd better tell Bruce. As department chair, he should know about this."

Catching Bruce outside his office, I showed him the letter and the postcards. "Nasty," he said. "What did you do to get this guy upset?"

"What did I *do*?" I said, my voice rising. "Published a fairly boring book!"

The next time I saw Sarah, I sat beside her on the studio floor and told her about the postcards and letter.

"Why, that's awful. How very nasty for you."

"But why would somebody do that to me?"

"This has got to be a very sick person. I don't think it's really about you. All you did was act like a professional, a grownup. It's an expression of his sickness."

"I hate it!" I said in a little-girl voice. "I hate it, hate it, hate it! It's just like before. He is doing disgusting things and I can't stop it. It makes me feel so helpless and small."

"I know. That's the way he wants you to feel, I suspect. Can you find a way to show how angry you are?"

"I don't know where to begin."

"Begin wherever you can."

Slowly, I moved onto the floor. I tried stomping with my feet, faster and faster until my heels were drumming the floor. I grunted nonsense syllables, "Gah! Poo! Na-na-na-na!" louder and louder. I got down on my knees and pounded the floor with my fists, tentatively. In a few minutes I was tired. I moved closer to Sarah.

"I feel disconnected. The anger isn't connected to any person or target. I feel I'm disconnected as I do it. And it scares me. I'm afraid I can't be close to you and be angry."

Sarah asked, "May I talk about the movement?"

"Please do."

"It seems developmental, like you're just figuring out how to be angry."

"Yeah, I guess so."

I moved again, this time pushing, pressing against the floor with extended arms, protesting. And then I remembered the photo of myself at age four, the forlorn-looking child in coveralls beside a big shingled house. I knelt and talked to her. "It's OK to be angry, little girl. Now you have someone big enough to hold, strong enough to be with it. I will still hold you. Myra couldn't hold the anger. But now I'm big enough and calm enough and I love you plenty. And Sarah is big enough." Then I hit the floor with open palms, making a lot of noise. The most satisfying move was to take a pillow by the corners and slam it on the floor over and over.

I went to Sarah and nestled there next to her legs. "Sarah, will you talk to the little girl about it?"

"It's not only OK to be angry, it's important. It will make you feel better and stronger. It will help you feel more right."

"Will it go on forever?"

"No, it won't. It feels like that but it gets smaller when you really do it."

"Will people hate me?"

"Some people have trouble with anger but others will honor you for where the anger comes from. You're brave to do this and it's very good."

"I'm surprised," I said, taking a deep breath. "I do feel better. It feels miraculous to be encouraged into anger. When I was little, my feelings didn't count. My little girl wants to ask a question."

"Well sure."

"I don't have to do it all at once, do I?"

"No you don't. Go at your own pace."

After therapy I took a hike for an hour and a half in the fall woods. The sun was going down already, and the mostly-bare branches were outlines against a golden sky. When I got home I sat down at the kitchen table to write and draw.

> *Trust is the best thing. How amazingly open and vulnerable I can be. I feel so buoyant, like taking a dose of tranquility and peace, my whole body affected by the change. Imagine being able to be in the world without constant fear and feeling of wrongness*
>
> *I look out at the world and it is sharp, clear, and beautiful—those leaves, that golden color, the pink hue of clouds, the warmth of late day's sun gilding the oaks. It is a privilege to be breathing in this world. My feelings flow from out to in, taking in people and things with beneficence and flowing back fully into my core, like the tide or like a breath.*
>
> *For the last three months I have been hugely inward. Absorbing Sarah's comfort and care like a thirsty little camel. I still need it. Knowing that, I now can open my eyes with gratitude.*

The next time we met in the studio, it was a cloudy gray day outside, typical November. "It's about trust," I said. "Can I show you my drawings about this?"

"Of course, I'd love to see them."

I pushed my sketchbook towards her. "Here's one where I drew three golden circles that intersect. Inside them," I read aloud, "'You can *always* come back,' 'I am *here* for you,' 'This is a *safe* place.' '*Always, Here, Safe*.' Little Jane feels so cared for and safe."

"Oh, I'm glad you feel that."

"I feel kind of shy about this, but look at this other drawing I did about trust. It's like a forest in winter. See how the brown trees arch up into a golden space with the word 'TRUST.' The ground supporting them is FAITH. It feels like faith in the process and in myself."

"I see—in between you wrote '*witnessing, touch, little girl can ask her own questions, tender, doors opened inside, all of me here to be seen, I ask for what I need.*' It's very true. Trust is the basis, Faith is the basis, this is the most important thing. It's a beautiful drawing."

I let out the breath I had been holding. No matter how many times I took a chance to show Sarah my feelings, a risk was still a risk.

"I'm still pretty amazed to have you here in the studio. When I talk to my dance friends they always say 'Wow' when I say I've invited my therapist into the studio. They know how vulnerable and open that is."

MORE OBSCENE LETTERS and postcards arrived at work. After the first ones, I approached the faculty mailboxes warily each day, and then I asked Roberta to take out the suspicious mail and keep it in a box in her office. One slipped by, a simple white business envelope with a hand-written return address for a Dr. Levy at Syracuse. "You fraud..." it began, and followed up with references to God and sex and women, bewildering in their lack of logic. I immediately suspected it was not from the actual Dr. Levy, who had recently published an article in *Science* magazine.

I soon found out that the anonymous writer was sending obscene letters and postcards purporting to be from me to other faculty who contributed to the book I edited, as well as to others who had published in *Science* magazine, to a woman columnist at University of Connecticut, and apparently at random to other scientists, particularly women, around the country.

I appealed to the college president's office for support, making call after call to his assistant and getting few responses.

Then came the voicemail messages from security departments at universities across the country. "Uh, Professor Rowan? This is chief security officer Joseph Larkin from the University of Colorado. Would you please call at your earliest convenience? My phone is ..."

"Hello, this is Jane Rowan returning your call."

"Ah, yes, Dr. Rowan." His voice dropped to a low register. "Dr. Carlson in our Chemistry Department received a card from you, with obscene and threatening contents."

"Oh, God. I didn't send that card."

He cleared his throat. "It's my job to protect our faculty. The card had your return address, and we are prepared to take action...."

I fumbled to explain and sound professional, while my heart raced and I felt shamed and helpless. The officer finally signed off with unsatisfied mumblings.

These phone calls were oddly reassuring. The security departments at some institutions were taking the harassment very seriously and trying to protect their faculty. I'd informed our security chief, Spencer Barkin, but he said only, "The best thing to do is ignore it." I called him again after the third call from outside security guys.

"Do you know who it is?" he asked.

"No."

"Well then, there's no use trying anything."

It was a week or so after that exchange that Roberta called to me from her desk, "I think I got something for ya."

I walked into her office a bit warily. "Mmm?"

"I think I got a nail on this guy's handwriting. Look at this FAX—you see? It's from an applicant for the chemistry position, some guy at a community college in Texas. It sure looks to me like that writing is the same."

"It looks like it could be. You are a much better reader of handwriting than I."

"I think we need to get Spencer to give it to a handwriting expert."

"God, yes. Maybe we have a clue." I let out a long breath. "That would be amazing. Roberta, you are so swift!"

After a certain amount of phone tag, Spencer agreed to take the new specimen and present it with some of the postcards to an expert. It came back a match.

"Wow, what can we do now?" I asked Spencer.

"Well, I still don't think it's a good idea to stir the waters. But if you want to take it up, you need to go to the president first."

I called my friend Marianne, who had been so supportive in hearing about my early abuse. She was a professor as well, so she would understand how devastating it was to be attacked this way at the workplace.

"My god! That's appalling. What can you do about it?"

"Well, wait. I want to talk a bit more about its impact and how I'm feeling." It felt good to say that out loud. Too many colleagues at work couldn't sit still to listen to my feelings. They jumped in very quickly with "fix-it" suggestions. Often their rush to advise me made me feel that I shouldn't express my dismay. And then their advice sounded like a lot of imperatives—You should track him down. Did you call the police? Have you called the FBI? You should sue him. When I had to say, "No, I have not called the FBI," then I felt inadequate.

"OK, talk," Marianne said in her short, direct style.

"I feel like my reputation is being raped."

"Well it is! Not that people who know you will believe any of this, but it does associate you with obscenity."

"It makes me feel so helpless! I hate that. I feel like a kid all over again, and a man is doing things to me and I can't stop him."

"Yes, naturally it brings up the feelings from the abuse."

"I feel shamed even though I didn't do anything."

"It's not your fault. You really need to take action here."

"Wait. I think there's a limited amount I can do. Can we talk some more about how it affects me and why?"

"One thing that comes to me," she said, "is that sexual shaming has been used against women for a long time, associating us with dirty sexuality. And we both know that humiliation has been used against women who tried to make it in male professions."

"Ah. Women in science and all that." I liked this analysis but it started to feel awfully rational. "But I don't want to feel all these childish feelings of powerlessness and fear."

"Of course you don't. Let's think about what you can do. You really have to get the college to act."

"Believe me, I'm trying." Marianne started to tell me what to do and I began to drift away.

IN THE LARGE SPACE of the dance studio, a dozen of us were moving, each with eyes closed. I was participating in another weekly movement group with Rita as leader. That night I stamped my feet on the floor, first deliberately and then faster and faster until it felt like a fierce spirit had taken over my body. I spit nonsense syllables out of my mouth, my face wrinkled into a mask of anger and disgust. I drummed loudly on the wall with my palms. I felt satisfied and powerful. The movements felt completely necessary and correct.

After the movement session, we had time for art work. I took a lump of clay and began kneading it. I pushed and prodded it with my thumb. Suddenly I knew it was a sea monster. The thumb prints had become waves that made a spreading mane while the bulk of the clay needed a snarling face. It grew fangs and squinting glaring eyes. My emerging beast was still in the process of being born from the waves. I loved it.

In my turn in our sharing circle, I said, "I really needed to be furious. Stuff has been going on at work that is just crazy-making. So I pounded and made noise. And look what came to me in the forming time..." There was a collective ah... from the group, very satisfying.

Rita was about to share what she had seen of my movement. She moved toward the wall and raised her arms, then stopped and asked, "Is it OK to show this?"

"Yes," I said. "Thank you for asking." She pounded on the wall. It looked strong and sure to me.

I DIDN'T WANT TO go to Pam's house but I had made a date. I walked up her front steps and rang the bell. "Come on in," she called. "How are you, sweetie."

"I'm not doing well," I said and I told her about the harassment.

"That's horrible. You don't deserve that. What a nut case!" She listened attentively for a little while. Then she began a long complaint about her dog's behavior. Her dog's behavior problems?! *Please, I think this harassment deserves a bit more attention than that!*

By contrast, my next movement session with Pam was cathartic. As we talked before dancing, she started giving me advice, but I said, "Let's just move."

After we both warmed up, Pam approached me and pointed at her breastbone. "Press here and I will fight for you. Who should I attack? I'm ready."

"The guy in Texas, for sure!"

We both air-punched and kicked the harasser from Texas with viciousness and humor. It felt terrific.

ONE SATURDAY IN mid-November, Helen and I met at my house for a cup of tea before taking a hike in the woods. Reluctantly, I hauled out a manila envelope and asked Helen to look at some of the ugly cards I had received. I needed witnessing. I wanted someone else to see how disturbing these cards were.

"Oh, sickening. They are venomous. Confusing, too. They don't make sense."

"No, that's part of it. They feel crazy."

"They are crazy as well as hateful. He must be a very disturbed man."

Helen and I started off in her car to go hiking, but I was crying hard.

"Do you want a hug?" she asked.

"Uh-huh," I said.

She pulled over to the side of the road and just held me for a long time while I sobbed on her shoulder.

"I was supposed to be safe in my good-girl professional side of life! It's so bewildering. It makes no sense, the words, the feelings, the hatred."

"No, it doesn't make sense. It's not really about you—it's his craziness."

"It just takes me right back to being little and helpless and feeling shamed."

"Well, sure it does. But it doesn't mean you have anything to be ashamed of."

"Thanks. Thank you for just letting me cry. I really needed that. We can go on now."

When we got to the parking lot at the start of the trail, the area was swarming with pickup trucks and guys with guns.

"Oh my god. Hunting season for birds." I felt scared and vulnerable.

"Oh, damn. You're right," Helen said.

"It should be OK but I don't feel OK."

"That's fine. I'm not happy hiking around hunters either. Let's go on to the trail by the Clear River."

The other trail was free of hunters and we hiked safely.

≈ 26 Webs

My sabbatical was about to end in January. I walked up the stairs to my office lugging my briefbag with a load of course materials. Today I needed to clean up the lab space and I hoped to get some of my reserve books into the library.

"Can I talk to you for a minute?" one of my colleagues asked. He wanted me to take on a student who needed help.

"Do you have a minute?" one of the students asked when she saw me in the lab.

"Would you be on the exam committee?" my department chair asked.

It felt like an endless series of demands. And the harassment was still going on, cards arriving at irregular intervals. How could I re-enter this workaday world?

The next time I saw Sarah, I told her how it felt.

"I know. It's a lot, but you'll do OK. You have before."

"I want to remember how precious this fall has been. It's done but it's not gone—I want the little girls to know that."

"Yes, it's been very special. Not everybody can go as deep as you do. It's really wonderful to work with you. I learn from you."

"Mmm. Thanks. That makes me feel good. But the little ones are scared that I'll leave them. Let me talk to them directly." I sat very close to Sarah on the studio floor and held a pillow, feeling I was holding Little Jane. I spoke to this little girl softly. "I won't be there every second but I'm really going to be a good Mommy for you. I'm not going to go away. It's very important to me to have this work go on."

Then Sarah told me that she was going away for a vacation the next week.

"No!" I said. "Not now."

"I really need the time now. I'm sorry I didn't plan better and let you know in advance."

After our session was over it really hit me that she was leaving. I alternated between gratitude for the wonderful work we'd been doing and fury at her timing.

The next morning as I was sitting with Little Jane before going to work, I felt overwhelmed by my need for Sarah. How could I meet that need in her absence? Maybe I could find a place to meet her in my imagination. Could Sarah be a school counselor at my elementary school? But no, it didn't feel safe enough at the red-brick school I went to. Where would be a place to meet safely?

I saw a little cabin in the woods. It was up the hill from the house where I grew up, behind the school in a patch of forest where I had often played. I led Little Jane by the hand and we walked up the path. There it was, a log cabin.

We walked up the steps and knocked on the brown unpainted door. The door opened and there was Sarah. She was older than Little Jane's parents. She knelt down and looked at us. Her eyes were brown and kind. She said, "Welcome. You can come in whenever you're ready."

The cabin was warm inside. The whole space was open with cushions and a wood floor, windows and trees close by.

"Here is a place," she said, "where the rules you learned don't apply. You don't have to be nice or be quiet. You are welcome to cry or scream. It's safe to throw things and be wild. You can write on the walls and it will magically be erased when you are done. It's OK to be angry here, too. And there's a magic rocking chair in the corner where we all can sit together. I'll always be here whenever you want me."

Little Jane felt welcome right away. She adopted that cabin and returned to it often.

THE UGLY CARDS KEPT coming. Every few weeks I went into Roberta's office, took a deep breath, and asked to see the latest. "Your book sucks. All you did is sleep your way into a career. You should go back to the kitchen, you lezbo." Some of them ranted about creationism and Jesus.

"You tuna-crotch, shit-for-brains bitch. You suck. PS, Fuck you." That was the worst of them, its images sticking like slime in my mind.

I persisted in trying to get help from the college. On the one hand, the security chief and the president's office told me that they would be in charge of investigating and taking action. On the other hand, they stalled and did nothing.

A couple of months after Roberta had identified the handwriting, after I had written memos and made numerous phone calls to the president's office, the president's assistant finally lined up a call to the college's attorney. I sat in her small beige office while she held the phone and I listened on the speakerphone. It soon became clear she hadn't even read my memos carefully.

I heard the attorney say that obscene cards were not necessarily a crime, just a nuisance.

"I see," said the assistant.

"Wait!" I interrupted, receiving a glare. "It's not just that these are obscene and distressing—it's also that he is sending dozens of these messages to other faculty across the country, claiming they're from me."

"Well, that could be a case of fraud. You might have something there," the lawyer's voice said from the speakerphone.

"But can't we do anything directly, like asking the police department in his town to check this guy out? He could be harassing and scaring staff and students at his college, too."

"We'll have to see. Let me see if I can find an attorney in Texas that we can work with."

After a good deal of arm-twisting ("You don't really want to stir this guy up. Leave it alone and he'll get tired of it." "He hasn't yet, and it's been months!"), I persuaded Spencer the security guy to take the matter to the local police. We lugged the large box of papers—dozens of cards and letters, copies of letters sent to other institutions, and a bulk of magazines and offers, obscene and not, that had come to me. Evidently the harasser filled out postcards for adult-only videos, Playboy magazine, or anything else that came his way with, "Dr. Roan, Scientists Who Believe, College, Town, State" and send them in. Always my name misspelled in the same way, always the "Scientists Who Believe" line.

So we carried the heavy box to the local police station, where we were met by a middle-aged, very non-committal policeman and a younger female detective. Spencer did most of the talking, man-to-man, but I got in a few words.

"I'm afraid there's nothing illegal about this," the male detective said.

"Not stalking, not discriminatory harassment?" I asked.

"Were there any places where he threatened you with bodily harm?"

"Not spelled out, but it's pretty threatening."

"I agree it's nasty," said the female detective. Watching her expressions, I felt she was torn between wanting to take a tough-guy stance in solidarity with her teammate and feeling some sympathy for me and revulsion at the mailings. "But I don't see a crime either. Maybe you could pursue it through the civil courts, for defamation and for stealing your identity."

Oh, great! the civil courts—toothless, endless, and besides, they'll probably try to make me *look crazy.*

"Could you get in touch with the local police in Texas and just feel out the situation?"

"Oh, no, we can't do that," the male police officer said.

Bullshit, you can't. I'm sure you do things like that all the time.

I left the cold brick police station and headed out to my car, shaking with rage and helplessness. When I got home I called Roberta, the secretary, to update her on the latest frustrations.

"Thank you so much for your help with this."

"Just doing my job," she said.

"It's way beyond doing your job, and you know it."

"For you, it's worth it."

When I got off the phone, I cried over that. *This is what support feels like. I wonder why it seems so rare with my colleagues.*

I DECIDED THAT I would feel less powerless if I went to see a lawyer on my own. I chose a local attorney who had a good reputation with civil liberties and gender issues. He met me in the late afternoon in March, almost six months after the cards had started. His office was simple, his manner friendly and straightforward.

After I laid out the basics, I asked him what I could do.

"Well, it's very ugly. Unfortunately, I have to agree that the obscene cards themselves are not a criminal matter."

"Maybe not, but it feels like stalking to me."

"However, his sending cards in your name is identity theft and worse. We could certainly make a case that he has damaged your reputation. You'd need to provide evidence of actual damage, perhaps records of therapy." That was certainly a frightening thought, bringing my records of trauma into a courtroom.

"We could try a civil suit," he continued. "How to identify the writer for sure and link him with the cards—that's an issue."

"The college is supposed to be making contact with a lawyer in Texas to check out his local reputation. And to write a cease-and-desist letter."

"That's a good move. It would put him on notice."

"Maybe they'll get some more information we could go on. It's hard doing it from a distance, although I'm glad he's not here. I wish the police here would be more help."

"Yes, it's hard without the backup. Maybe we should wait a bit and see what the college lawyers turn up."

"I suppose so," I sighed.

In short, it ground on. Getting help from the college felt like wrestling taffy. I think if I encountered a similar situation now, I would do more on my own, disregarding the college's condescending limitations.

AFTER I GOT OVER the shock of coming back from sabbatical, I remembered how much I loved the classroom. I was teaching biochemistry, one of my favorite courses.

One morning I was demonstrating how a protein molecule folds into a specific shape. I scrunched my whole body into a ball and waved my hands to show where the action was. A small observing part of me thought, *You might look silly, but it works.* In other classes, I openly shared my wonder at complexities of carbon bonding and the marvels of the chemical compounds that plants produce. The students responded to my enthusiasm and the classes felt lively and congenial.

Standing in a new class with a horseshoe ring of students seated around me, I noticed how feelings and personalities seemed to enter through my skin right into my heart. I described the syllabus and the requirements and the group work, while noting students looking down or gazing at me with deer-in-the-headlights intensity. A boy slouching in the back, a girl talking nervously to me after class about her learning disability.

I was called to do much. Each new advisee who walked into my office presented a whole life open to my view. Each student in my classes brought feelings, cognitions, and social dynamics.

I didn't want to shut out the richness of the demands of teaching. But I wondered how I could be with my own needs as well. Going back and forth between these places was like bungee jumping.

Could I see the two aspects as related? I had certain gifts of seeing the students in their whole lives, of smelling resistance and difficulty, of intuiting how to guide. Sensitized as a child, I was a woman alive to the richness of these lives crowding mine.

"It sounds like your little girl gets to be there quite a bit," Sarah said when I shared these thoughts with her.

"Yes. She's not only a distressed little girl. She does have fun sometimes."

THE HARASSMENT NEVER had a clear resolution. After about a year, the cards stopped, while the obscene magazines tapered off more slowly. For a long time it was an ugly cloud that I pushed to the back of my mind. I didn't want to talk to anyone about it. When I did, people asked me how I brought on or what I did to resolve it. They seemed to be blaming the victim.

Finally when I wrote about it for this memoir, the ugliness detached from the lining of my psyche. In a weekly women's writing workshop, I described the postal abuse. The other writers' responses of breath-held silence and vocal sympathy at last opened my soul. It was not my fault, any more than the original abuse was the fault of the four-to-six year old.

Sarah and I watched it all go up in flames. I had brought the packet of cards and letters I had held onto these past six years. We were in her small office with the wood stove, the snowy hemlocks outside the windows.

"I need help with this," I said. "I'm trying to write about the harassment, and I end up feeling scared again."

"It was a hard time," she affirmed.

"I kept some of the letters. They are here in this packet."

"I wonder why you kept them," she said.

"Why? Well there was a part of me that still needed the evidence on hand to show it really happened."

Webs

the hill in morning fog
all about love hate
every leaf and branch drenched
no understanding his motive
mist at the top ovenbird
obscene malicious meanwhile
cries *teacher teacher teacher.*
wrestling with love and trust.
hermit thrush pours clear liquid song
what could I make of him did I hate
over it all jeweled moss lichen-softened stone
furious yes baffled why he wrote
the spider-webs
tuna-crotch shit-for-brains bitch
pouches of cloud in the branches
not my hatred his sickness.
come close see miniscule architecture
hold it with two sticks
tiny struts tension wires lit by moisture
not drop it not be fouled by it
and the spider yellow gray waiting.

"That makes sense. When you were little there was no evidence."

"So this time I have the evidence—See? It really happened. See? He really said, 'Women scientists suck. You should all go sell real estate.'"

"And many other ugly things."

"Yes. I think I'm ready to let it go, though. I think I'm ready to burn the letters."

We sat on the floor in front of the wood stove. She creaked the iron doors open. There were faintly glowing embers inside.

I pulled out one of the cards and read out loud, "Science sucks and so do you. You pathetic excuse for a scientist."

I wadded it into a ball, tighter, tighter, then tossed it into the woodstove. It did nothing for a moment, then uncurled, produced toxic smoke—*oh no, I want flames!*—then finally popped into a small sheet of flame. I watched it all the way into a frail shell of gray, with orange shadows flickering over the uneven surface. "Ah. That is satisfying."

The next one, more ranting about women in science, about Jesus. Into the fire.

Several more, with incoherent sentences on creationism sprinkled with personal insults. Into the stove.

Finally, "You tuna-crotch, shit-for-brains bitch..." I took a deep breath and wadded it tightly, pushing on it with my palms. Into the fire. I held my breath as it writhed, then burst into a flare of light.

"It's beautiful. Transformed. It has been made light," I said. "I never was able to catch him in the real world, but this helped to burn his slimy words out of my psyche."

Sarah looked at me with something like pride as well as warmth.

I watched as tiny worms of orange ember crawled around the gray folds of burned paper. I breathed again.

Heading for the Light

≈ 27 But Why?

WHAT KEPT ME ATTACHED to the mother and father who had betrayed me? I cherished my family heritage of values, intellect, curiosity, books, technical skills, mathematics, and politics. Then there was my still-living, still-vexing mother. I was held in place both by the many good things and by the powerfully interlocking, closed system that was my family. To pull away from their world-view felt like pulling roots from the soil, a messy and risky operation.

I WAS MAKING my decaf coffee and getting the milk from the refrigerator, thinking about going to work one morning in the summer, with the barrage of harassment still close. Suddenly I felt heavy blue desolation in my ribcage and a dizzy foreboding. Abandoning my breakfast, I sat in the rocking chair in the living room and hugged a pillow, while wails tore out of me. After the sobs slowed down I asked, "What is it, Little Jane?"

A fragment of picture invaded my mind, while I rocked in my chair. With oily pastels I drew a picture of the image, then taped a flap of paper over it so that I could flip through my sketchbook without having to confront it. For days I dragged around exhausted.

I met Sarah in the studio, the windows open to distant traffic sounds. "Oh, god, I had a new memory," I said. "It's a visual one. Would you hold me?"

"Of course." She opened her arms and held me while I sobbed convulsively.

"I see a pink-purple swollen object close to me at eye level. Oh yuck!" I gasped and cried again. Sarah handed me more Kleenex and made soothing sounds. "And there are some reddish curly hairs springing from skin just a little further away. It's so awful!"

"Oh, poor little one. This is so hard."

"It's disgusting! I'm so confused. I thought it would help if I had a visual memory. But I don't see the room where this is happening. I don't see the person attached to this thing. Jack's beard was reddish, but I don't see his face here, just these curly hairs. Ooh!"

I knew right away that Sarah believed me. It wasn't like trying to tell Myra. I felt Sarah's warmth right there with me. She continued to hold me as I said the same words over and over, as I cried and was silent and cried again.

After a while, I wanted Sarah to speak to Little Jane. She said, "I believe you, little one. You're really brave to come and tell me. I'm happy you trusted me enough to tell me that memory, even though the memory itself is awful."

Sitting next to Sarah on the floor, I spoke to the child, also. "I believe you, little one. Utterly, all the way down to the bottom. I love you anyway."

Sarah said, "Remember, the little girl can control the memories somewhat. And she doesn't have to keep having them in order to convince me and Big Jane. We know she's telling the truth."

I snuggled up close to Sarah again and she stroked my hair. After a few minutes I felt everything relax inside me.

Trust. How can I possibly say what it means to lie here, touched, safe, separate, feeling your warmth. My boundaries dissolve and yet they don't.

Yes, it's important to see Jack in my mind and accuse him. But trust—so sweet, so basic. It is the air I need to breathe in order to do this work.

A few minutes later, I looked up at Sarah. She sat with head bowed, eyes closed. I saw the wrinkles on her face. I felt sure she was quiet inside and feeling compassion. It looked so simple, but I thought it must take enormous skill and strength just to be present for a person, not to fix it or hurry to the next stage, just to hold and let be. I felt as naked as an oyster, open and defenseless.

In the next studio sessions, I writhed on the floor and gagged, wholly inside the little girl's body-experience. I had to bypass the language problem. When Jack did this to me, I was about three to six years old, certainly talking, but I didn't have words for the things that happened or for the overwhelming feelings that they evoked. When I tried to use language, there was no way to translate.

"How could anyone do that to a little girl?" I asked Sarah. "How could *Jack* do that to *me*? I just can't get over the contradictions—my fear and my love. How confusing it was."

"So confusing."

"And it hurts so much inside my heart! He broke it. Impossible to believe. I mean, he was such a man of principle. He talked women's equality and he rationalized being led by his prick.

"It's too much! It's not fair," I said in an angry-child voice. "*He* should be hurting. *He* should be having to do the work and face what he did and how huge it was."

"Yes, it's hard to know what to say to the little girl about that. It's very unfair and he was selfish," she said.

"Very selfish. He made excuses for himself. It wasn't true that he couldn't stop." My voice rose to a scream. "That was his *excuse*!"

I took a long, sobbing breath. "There's no explaining. And there's no making it go away! Even when I take care of Little Jane, I know the abuse happened and I can't make it not happen."

"Unfortunately, that's true."

"I know that he said he couldn't stop himself. He claimed that men have uncontrollable urges."

"He lied. Maybe he lied to himself."

"How could he not know how terrified I was?" I asked Sarah, in the quiet of the studio. "I still don't know how he could do that to his own little girl. How could he not stop?"

"It is a mystery. But he was a very selfish and self-centered man."

"Sarah, I hate being frightened like this. It just doesn't feel good. In the past I've gone hiking and camping alone where some of my friends think I'm nuts. I take risks. I like that feeling of freedom."

"I know you do."

"I feel so scared now. Will I always be fearful? I like the old way, being fearless."

"I think you'll go back to having a high threshold for fear. This won't last forever."

"I guess I need to learn to live with it. But I don't want to. It's awful, I hate it!"

"You need to for the little girl's sake. It's a part of you."

THE NEXT TIME I saw Sarah, I felt confused and frightened. "Last night when I was home, something hard came up."

"Uh-huh?"

"I was sitting with the little girls and I got a lot of sexual feelings. At the same time I felt queasy. *His* fingers were there touching me. I told the little girl that her feelings were all OK, but whose feelings are these?" I sat quiet for a minute or so, staying with this unease, but I felt stuck. Nothing shifted.

"I don't know what to do," I said.

Sarah asked, "Do you want to hear anything like interpretations about those feelings?"

"OK, try it," I said. I felt spacey but I could hear her voice from a distance.

"Your body responds to touch even when you're really little. Even when the touch is wrong and inappropriate, your body responds. It doesn't mean you're bad or that you encouraged it or participated in it." I stored that thought away.

"But also, I'm afraid if I say, 'Stop it,' all touch will go away. If I say stop it, everything will be broken, my family will break. But most of all, I can't sort out about wanting to say *stop it* to him and still having my feelings and still wanting touch."

"The little girl does not have to be alone with this now. One terrible thing he did was to make the little girl experience sexual feelings in isolation, very alone."

"Yeah. I felt so lonely and confused."

"It's not about losing your sexuality by saying 'stop it.' It's about regaining it as your own."

I DREAM OF FLYING. I'm in a tiny airplane with an open cockpit, alone. The plane is bright yellow. I enjoy flying above the scenery, above the highways near Seattle, over the green landscape and highways.

Another flying dream. I'm in the same kind of plane, bright red, and I'm in a university library, zooming around above the wooden bookshelves and catalogs. I love the feeling of flight, the airborne, curving sensations.

Vivid sensations of flying came to me on ordinary days—dizzy, looping. My whole body felt the pull, the sense of spinning and looping, or of pulling backwards rapidly.

I told Sarah, "I think the little girl used this flying dissociation to get away during the mouth-rape."

"Yes, that sounds exactly true. She did what she needed to do. And the library scene is a perfect metaphor—she's zooming around above, not touching the knowledge that is right there."

"MOM, I'M COMING UP next week," my son Will said on the phone, "and I want to stay with you."

"Great!" I said, and felt happy that he was coming but also apprehensive. I was deep inside my inner work.

I told Sarah that Will was coming. "I think I need to tell him about the abuse."

"Yes," she said, "I think it's time."

"I know I need to be ready and to have some extra space for him, not just dump it on him."

"It *is* his grandfather."

"Yeah." I paused, remembering a scene at Myra's house, "and Will told me recently that he missed Jack."

"What did he miss, I wonder?"

"He told me he missed Jack's teaching about electricity and how things worked. He really was a good teacher. I miss him sometimes, too." I paused. "It's so damned complicated! But I think I really want to tell Will now. I wasn't ready before."

"It could bring you closer to him," she said.

"Well, that would be nice, if it happens."

The next day I picked Will up at the train station. We made dinner together and I asked about his work and his friends. Later, after a game of Scrabble, we settled on the living room couch to talk.

I took a deep breath, glanced at his face, then looked down. "I think I'm finally ready to tell you what's been going on with me lately. You know... the family stuff... the therapy. I've have been having a hard time."

"Yeah, I noticed things didn't seem easy."

"Well, what it is..." I gulped air, "... Jack molested me when I was young. I didn't remember... I didn't understand my own memories until lately."

"Wow," he said slowly. "I wondered why you always seemed angry at him."

His insight stunned me. "Really?" I said.

"I have a lot of friends who are going through stuff like this. It seems pretty common. I'm sorry it happened to you."

"Oh." I had tears in my eyes. "I appreciate that. I know it's going to be a long process. I... I can't give you details now. I'll be able to tell you more sometime."

"Yeah, that's all right. I don't want any more right now." He looked at me, then away into the distance, his face serious and thoughtful. "I don't know what to say."

I didn't hear any doubt in his voice. I expanded inside as I realized the gift of his belief and respect.

"Sarah, I brought some pictures of Jack." We were sitting on the floor in the studio at the beginning of a session. "Trying to understand who he was."

"Oh, good. You know I love seeing photographs."

"Look at this one of Jack with my son. Don't they look sweet?" I handed her the color picture of the bald-headed man smiling beatifically, holding on his shoulder a sleepy infant in a blue terrycloth jumpsuit.

"Mmm. That is wonderful. He does look loving and proud."

"He was the one who held and cuddled me when I was little. Somehow I know that. My mother didn't cuddle, ever. I remember how she didn't hold Will when he was little."

"Not hold a grandbaby. That's really odd."

"That's really Myra," I sighed.

I handed her the picture where I was a toddler in Jack's arms, reaching out joyfully to him, totally at ease.

"Yes, you do look secure and he looks fond."

"But how can that be true? If he was that loving, he couldn't have done those things to me. I'm scared all over. I'm so afraid his reality will win, that he'll be right. Like he can deny it or deny that it hurt me, and that will make it so."

"This looks to me like a *before* picture. It's really possible that both things are true. He loved you but he did those things."

"I don't understand! I don't."

"Some things cannot be explained." She sighed and looked sad.

I sat thinking. "I'll never know how he carried it with him." Then I told Sarah about the time about a year before Jack died. He was in the nursing home and no longer able to walk. The Parkinson's was taking his mind, too, so he was hardly talking and sometimes he spoke more in images than a real conversation.

I had wheeled his chair into the day room for a while and was wheeling him back through the hall when he said in a low and shaky voice, "The pit."

I stopped the chair to lean over him and say, "The pit?'

He nodded a little. "Don't want to go." My mind formed the image of a swirling, perilous chasm.

"You're afraid of it?" I asked. He nodded again and looked down, agitated and shaking.

"I think we all have to go there. I think it will be OK," I told him, thinking he meant death. I kept trying reassure him as he slumped further into his wheelchair.

In the light-filled studio I said to Sarah, "It was an amazing conversation, given that he was so out of it. But now I wonder whether he meant hell, the fiery pit he was taught about as a Catholic kid, whether he was feeling his guilt."

"It could well be."

"Here's the big question, the one I can't get past," I said. "*How could he*? It's the problem of evil—how could a basically good and loving man do something so hideous?"

"I still don't know the answer to that. People do these things. Who knows what happened in his childhood."

"Yes, I've wondered that. I guess I'll never know."

≈ 28 Mothering

I PARKED MY CAR in the driveway and picked up some of my bundles—bakery bread, fresh flowers. Walking up the cement sidewalk, I noticed the summer's flowers dark brown on their dry stalks. I rang the doorbell to let Myra know I was there, paused a minute, then opened the wooden front door.

There she was, a small mousy woman in a print dress. Her face was sagging with the weariness of eighty-some years. This tiny woman loomed so large in my emotional world—it was uncanny. *Maybe I don't need her.* Then she smiled with genuine pleasure to see me, and I was swept into her world again.

I continued to be the dutiful daughter, once a month arriving on Friday, greeted by her love and distance, awaking Saturday in despair, working all day on her projects and priorities. As her blindness deepened, the projects took on more importance. In addition to putting storm panels in the doors, I needed to install bigger light bulbs and drive her to the store that specialized in equipment for the blind. I marked the controls of appliances in big bright markings and bought her a pair of matching programmable radios so she could listen to her favorite programs in the kitchen or the bedroom.

All day Saturday it was "just one more thing." Then on Sunday she would relax a bit and we would have a few minutes of conversation. That was when she might ask me a sudden series of questions about my work. I was often not inspired to say much, since her interest seemed belated.

It was one of those Sunday mornings. She was perched on the rust-colored couch and I was sitting on the floor. I told her about the two young girls I'd been babysitting a few times. "They are really cute. Rachel is quiet and sweet. Phoebe is fearless and totally social, will talk to strangers."

"It sounds like you are having fun taking care of them."

"Yes, I am." I paused and thought, then took a plunge. "Well, it's an interesting situation. They are staying with my friend Abby because their father is a molester."

"It seems like there is a lot of that going on these days," Myra said.

A dumbstruck, pondering silence on my side for nearly a minute as I sat and studied her face. It didn't give me any clues. *What am I going to say to this?*

Then she sat back a few inches and said, "I guess there always has been." Her face looked both sad and closed. *Oh my! I think she just communicated something to me.*

"Yes, I think that's true," I said firmly. *I wonder if we'll ever say it more directly.* There was a short silence, then we went on to something else.

I TOLD HELEN ABOUT the weekend that Sunday afternoon after I got home. We walked down a dirt road to our favorite reservoir, talking. "I just feel wiped out after these weekends. It's much more than the physical tiredness from driving and doing chores and then more driving."

"Well of course, her going blind and all the feelings that brings."

"Yeah, I feel really sorry for her, and amazed by her toughness in living alone."

"That is pretty strong of her."

"But then I have these intense, complicated feelings about her and the abuse. I get so angry, but this old woman isn't the one I'm angry at. But she is, too. And then when she acts helpless, is helpless, sometimes it makes me so mad, but I feel I shouldn't be angry. Especially because she's getting old and won't be around forever."

"It doesn't sound easy."

"I wish I could love her more. But it's complicated."

"For sure, it is complicated. Don't be too hard on yourself," Helen said kindly.

> *MYRA IS ALWAYS going to be my mother. She's always going to be manipulative, controlling, indirect, helpless, limited, narrow, smart, capable, careful. She does what she can. She loves according to who she is.*

A candle was burning on the table by Sarah's side as the autumn night came in early. I told her of my visit to my mother. "I need to get away from Myra and Jack, dismiss them, and move out before I can take new steps," I said.

"Yes, as long as you are in their force field, you can't," said Sarah.

"I know I focus on Myra because she transmitted a lot of the family rules to me, and she was the arbiter. But that makes me feel bad. A lot of what she transmitted was him, his point of view."

"But she was the point of contact. I see that."

"In Myra's eyes he was never right, but he also was never wrong. She was always irritated at him but she never could get out of the marriage or change anything, it seemed."

"A terrible gray area to live in. A terrible area to bring a child into."

"My mother never says she's angry. She has as many words for unexpressed anger as the Eskimos have for snow. Let's see," I counted off on my fingers, "she simmers, mulls, stews, fumes, frets, fusses, steams, but she never says, 'I'm angry.'" We laughed for a moment.

"But what about talking to Myra about the abuse?" I asked.

"What about it?"

"I want to but I don't want to. I feel I should. I'm not ready. But what if I'm still not ready and she dies? Is that all right?"

"It is all right," said Sarah. "And you may decide you don't ever want to talk to her."

"You mean I can just take care of myself?"

"Yes."

"In any case I don't have to do it now. I can just be here."

I found my way out of the thoughts about telling Myra and back into my own body. "Can I sit next to you and put my head on your lap?"

"Of course."

I curled next to Sarah and was quiet for a long time, while she stroked my hair. My whole body relaxed and became peaceful.

"Is it okay to do nothing, just take comfort and feel loved?"

"Taking comfort is not doing nothing—it's doing a lot. I'm proud of you. You worked hard to get here!"

I felt Sarah's warm acceptance, a loving presence throughout my body. I asked, "But is it possible, unconditional love?"

"I'm not perfect but I do love you just the way you are."

"You won't get impatient?"

"If I get impatient, that's my stuff," she said. "My love is really there and it really is for you the way you actually are. Little girls deserve unconditional love, really need and deserve it."

Some fisted thing in my stomach unclenched for the moment. "Wow. Yes. Little kids do deserve that kind of love. But it is very hard to believe for more than a minute at a time."

"Take all the time you need. We'll come back to it over and over."

MY STRESS AROUND the big grant escalated as we planned renovations. All the faculty were jockeying for larger lab spaces, with me in the middle. My colleague Rebecca pulled me aside in the hall one day. I was stunned when she said, "That's a dog-fight. They can't pay you enough to do what you're doing."

"Well, thanks!"

There were other unexpected gifts. One day a woman I didn't know walked into my introductory course where we were having a discussion. It made me nervous that she was sitting there taking notes on my teaching. As usual, I was encouraging all the students to participate. When I asked a female student to speak directly to a young man about his ideas rather than talking to me, the evaluator made another mark on her paper and smiled behind her hand.

After the class was over and students had drifted away, she told me that she'd been amused because I had exhibited every single interactive teaching strategy they were looking for—hence the smile. I bounced down the hall to my office.

MYRA'S WORLD WAS closing in as she was going deaf as well as blind, staying in her house all the time. After hiring a young woman to do the grocery shopping, she was managing everything else—the cleaning and cooking and regular chores, all by herself. In my October visit, I asked whether she wanted to go for a ride to see the masses of colored leaves—even with poor sight, she could take that in. "No, you just go out and do the errands. I'll stay in."

At Thanksgiving Myra seemed extremely tired and took a lot of naps. We had the traditional dinner for family on Thursday and then a special lunch for Suzie the day after with turkey sandwiches, gravy, and stuffing.

The next day Kathy and I spent the afternoon doing projects around the house, putting up a folding door and fixing the doorbell. I was grateful for her company in the chores. We noticed Myra's criticisms together and her appreciations, too—we were sisters! When Kathy left I felt sad. *I want more sister.*

Late on Saturday I spent about an hour listening to Myra. She talked about the many details of how hard it was to cope with increasing blindness, not being able to see recipes or markings on the stove. She was very tired and asked me about depression. "I wonder how I can get out of this dragging feeling." I wondered whether it was physical or emotional, but I could only ask so much before she'd cut me off and change the subject.

"You're a good listener," she said at the end of our conversation, surprising me with her directness.

I left for home that day even though Myra had asked me to stay longer. I was crying as I drove up the ramp to the interstate. Then I plugged in a recording of East Indian devotional music and my spirit soared. *I am so joyful, I am so glad my life is mine! My life is mine.*

I told Sarah about the ups and downs of the weekend. "She's so needy of attention, like a child sometimes. Her emptiness is not mine to fill, right?"

"Right."

"Myra asked me what to do about her depression."

"Maybe she could take drugs. There are some very helpful drugs these days. I've known a lot of people who have been helped that way. I wonder if you could talk to her about that."

Startling. Who would Myra be if she were not depressed? But when I left the session and was driving home, feelings were buzzing inside like angry bees.

The next time I saw Sarah, I arrived confused and angry. "I think I'm angry at you for suggesting that Myra get drugs. It seemed like you just wanted to fix her, but I wanted you first to hear how hard it is and how I'm involved with her."

"I was just trying to..."

"Oh, please, don't say that!"

"I wish you wouldn't snap at me."

I was so frightened when she said that, I had a sensation of zooming backwards at a hundred miles an hour, back through the back of the couch where I was sitting. "I'm finding it really hard to stay here—I'm zooming away," I said.

"Oh, we need to pay attention to that," she said gently and with concern. "Can you tell me about it?"

"Well, I'm zooming backward really fast." I paused to try to find words. "I guess I'm scared that you are mad at me. I hope we can do this OK."

"I'm not angry at you. It's OK. I'm here and I'm not going away."

BUT I WASN'T DONE with anger yet. At home when I sat with my little girl, she was again terrified that Sarah wouldn't listen, that she'd make suggestions and try to fix everything. I told Sarah at our next session, "It's like I need to redo my whole anger landscape. In my family anger was unspoken. I zoom away, distance myself. I hold on to my anger and nurse it, just as my parents did. I don't tell you why I'm angry at you because then it loses its power. I'm scared you'll say, 'Oh, you shouldn't be angry about that. I was just...'"

"Yes," she said. "I see why you have those fears. It's fine for you to be angry with me. It's reasonable given what you perceived, and anyway anger doesn't have to be reasonable."

"It doesn't?" I laughed tremulously.

"I can see why you reacted to my saying, 'I was just trying to...' I was talking to the grownup, but it was the little one who needed to be heard."

And then she said hesitantly, "I'm not saying it's easy or fun to receive the anger, but it's part of my job."

That felt real and trustworthy.

"I also remember when I was in therapy and needed to be angry. It was really hard, and scary. And I needed to do a lot of it."

"Oh."

"And I'm not going to run away from feelings, the way Myra did."

I moved closer to her and put my head in her lap, feeling the comfort and safety.

After a few minutes I moved out onto the studio floor, sitting and yelling and pounding the floor. I was talking to Myra, "You're not listening! You don't want to hear. You tell me that the hurt must have happened by my fault on the bathtub. That is awful! It is wrong to mess with my mind like that."

"But maybe I never said it in words to Myra," I said to Sarah, my stomach curdling. "Maybe I shouldn't be mad at her."

"But you showed her really clearly the best you could," Sarah said, "and it's likely you were warned not to tell so you did it without words. And besides, she knew you were injured—she helped wash you."

"She had to try really hard not to understand! She was really, really working to *not* listen. She was being so scared and taking care of him and herself, but not me. I was the little one. I deserved the care and listening. I get so angry even now when she acts helpless, helpless, helpless."

Suddenly I loved seeing Little Jane be angry. I said out loud to her, "We still love you, in fact we love you especially when you're getting angry. You have every right to be mad and anyway little girls get to have feelings."

"Uh-huh!"

"But Sarah, I feel kind of ashamed and embarrassed about being angry at you so often. Is it really OK?"

"Yes, it is. Don't try to make this be over too soon. Your little girl has a lot to be angry at and it takes a long time to go through it."

Entering Sarah's home office on a brisk December day, I peeled off my scarf and coat and hung them by the door. I told her, "It's the end-of-semester crunch. I woke early today and couldn't go back to sleep. When I sat with the little girl this morning, I kept getting distracted by thoughts about politics at work and the needs of different students. Little Jane got mad and made me focus for a while, but then I got distracted again."

"Yes, that's understandable—both parts of it, the distraction and the little one's desire for attention."

Rapt

Little one,
I want to hold you
fiercely
with such delicacy
close wrapped, as open as sky
wail loudly, sigh inaudibly
protect you always
have you guide me
this song of surrender
these syllables of fire
this whisper of together.

"I see Little Jane has two mommies now—Big Jane and you. Because she's the custodial mommy, Big Jane has a hard job—constant care while doing all those other things. In some ways you have an easier job just seeing her once or twice a week."

"That's true," Sarah chuckled. "But Big Jane's job is to be good enough, not perfect."

"But I get so frustrated," I said in a little-girl voice, "when Big Jane just doesn't listen."

Sarah asked, "Can I speak to Little Jane?" This was a new intervention.

"Sure," I said.

"Big Jane is really busy right now doing things to earn a living and ultimately to take care of you. She really wants to be with you, she really cares for you, and this is a busy time. This happens to grownups. She will be there, she really will."

≈ 29 The Voice of Authority

THE CROWD CARRIED ME in a current from the train and left me beached on the shore of Grand Central Station. Clumps of people waited or greeted in the tawny, echoing space around the central information kiosk. I chose a spot and planted myself and my suitcase, not surprised that Will was late.

When I spotted his tall frame sloping through the bustle, I was relieved. I could have made it to his Brooklyn loft on my own on the subways, but seeing him I felt anchored despite the vastness of the city.

"Hi, Mom." He hugged me briefly and I felt his spark of gladness.

"Wow, nice hair!" I said, eyeing the stark blond color that contrasted his dark eyebrows. Will's hair, beard, and mustache changed nearly every time I saw him.

The next day we walked into the city over the great curve of the Williamsburg bridge, buffeted by cold winds and dodging bicycles on the walkway. The river spread out below us with a panorama of factories and housing projects, green parks and gray asphalt. We walked endlessly through the small streets of lower Manhattan, my short legs moving fast to keep up with his long ones. We explored several edgy art exhibits at tiny avant-garde museums.

"What did you think of that exhibit?" I asked after one with cartoons of flying body parts.

"Disturbing, the violence of the images," he said.

"Phew, you named it." We had a comfortable pace of discovery and reflection.

"I'm tired," I said finally.

"I'll take you to my favorite place to hang out," and he dodged into a narrow side street, then led me up a short flight of brownstone steps to the Tenants' Union Bookshop, a large, lofty space with a huge selection of used books and a coffee shop.

As we sat with our lattes, I asked him about work. He was an independent consultant for firms needing software. "It's not easy piecing together a life that way," I said, watching his face, not wanting to sound critical. He looked interested, not defensive at the moment. I went on, "When I was growing up, Jack was always on the edge and Myra was trying to hold it together."

He paused, looked at me and then away. "Jack's my model for this," he said so softly that I had to lean forward to catch his words." He glanced at me again. "I really admired, uh, the way he held out and didn't work for the big companies. The way he ran his own shop and stayed independent."

"Yeah, that was important to him... or maybe I should say... I don't know. He had to go that way. Myra told me he got so angry when he worked for the corporations." I hoped I wasn't reinforcing unrealistic dreams in Will, but it was the truth.

Will's face lit up. "Like that. I really want to do things my own way. I admired him so much when I was little."

The shadow of my memories lay between us on the table. I knew I didn't need to speak of it at the moment. I sighed and said, "I guess I didn't know how much you looked up to him."

"Yeah... the way he did it. Not like my dad's dad, the corporation man—not that I didn't love him, too. But Jack was special and what he did inspired me."

"I like seeing that in you," I said. "You want to make your own life, not go along. It's a hard life, but you're making it."

"But I didn't idealize Jack," he said. "He was difficult, too."

"Like his temper?"

"Yeah. That was scary." His eyebrows flared and his mouth turned down as he remembered.

SARAH AND I WERE sitting in her office with the homey pictures on the wall. "I'm still feeling so fragile. I work every day with the anger, making lots of drawings and sitting with the little ones, and still I feel so fragile. I don't really know what to do. I feel kind of stuck."

"Could you try talking to the little girl about it?"

I tried, but nothing seemed to work. Sarah said, "We need to find out what the little girl needs to keep her safe. And what she's afraid of."

"What are you afraid of, little one?" I said to the pillow in my arms. "All I get is blankness and distress," I said to Sarah. "I want to say, 'I hate you,' but it feels too scary. I see the picture of me and Jack and the kitten when I was really little and safe and I don't want to say, 'I hate you.'"

"You don't want to lose the good stuff, you don't want to break it all."

"I just feel so stuck."

"Maybe you could imagine somebody coming from the outside to intervene in the situation. This person could teach Myra and Jack how to behave. Could it be your adult self?"

"Uh-uh. That doesn't work."

"Could it be a social worker? Me?"

"No, not big enough, not strong enough."

"Who can you imagine that is big and strong enough?"

I felt frustrated and fearful as nothing came to mind, then, "Oh yes, a policeman!" I sat and breathed for a minute as the image came clearer. "I can see him coming to the door. He pounds on the door of the house at Shell Beach where we lived when I was three or four. He's big and beefy and red-faced, a classic Irish cop.

"The policeman says to my father, 'I want to talk to you about your daughter, what you've been doing to your little girl.'"

Sarah asked, "What happens next?"

"First, Jack doesn't want to let him in, but the cop pushes by him. We all go into the living room and sit on different chairs. The policeman sits by Jack on the sofa. Myra sits next to them on a chair. You and I sit opposite them.

"The policeman says to Jack, 'I know what you've been doing I know you've been putting your fingers where you shouldn't put them. And you can't do that any more.'

"Jack tries to say, 'But I only.... But she didn't get hurt.'

"Each time, the policeman just says, 'No, it's wrong. You can't do that.'"

"Tell me more about this policeman."

"He isn't even friendly. He's big and red-faced in a blue uniform with shiny buttons and a nightstick. He's right and firm and powerful. He's not the one that cuddles me."

In the next days I replayed this scene over and over. I kept calling the policeman back and he kept saying to Jack, "That was bad and you can't do it anymore."

"But I didn't hurt her."

"Yes, it hurt her. Look how it hurts when she pees."

"It's not like she was raped."

"Yes, it is like that. How can she trust you if you do that?"

"But I didn't really hurt her."

"You are making me lose my patience. It did hurt her and scare her. What you did was wrong and bad."

"But men do it all the time. Men have these urges they have to satisfy."

"I told you, I'm getting angry. This is not OK."

Then I imagined the policeman saying to me as the little girl, "I'll stay here as long as you want."

"It's OK to ask you to stay?"

"Just as long as you want, until you are really safe."

"Do I have to be thinking about this all the time?"

"No, you should just be a little girl and be safe. It's my job to protect you and it's fine with me."

Gradually I saw the imaginary scene more completely. Little Jane loved that the policeman was big and not scared. She was reassured when he did not listen to excuses.

"Myra," the policeman said, "it is your job to protect Jane even if you are scared. You can't pretend it's OK because it's not."

"Yes!" Little Jane chimed in, "It's not my job to take care of Myra."

The policeman said to Jack, "I don't want any more lies. No lies."

Jack said, "But I..."

"But you *nothing*! It's time to stop acting like a little boy with excuses. It's time to be a grownup and take responsibility."

I loved having this new figure in the life of my imagination. But one day I realized that I was impatient and bewildered. "It's not all better," I said to Sarah. "I'm still very sad. And angry. Am I supposed to be all OK now? I feel I am bad or ungrateful for not being all better."

Sarah said, "This is only a part of the process. The process is long. It isn't just one step."

"I think one thing that was scary about learning to be angry was that I thought I had to be angry enough to make things change. It's not that way. The little girl doesn't have the power to change anything even when she gets angry. She needs a grownup to intervene."

"It's really true. You didn't have the power. You were very little."

IT WAS A COLD night and the windows of the Asian noodle restaurant were steamed up. I sat at a small table with my friend Heidi. I'd known her for more than ten years and liked her a lot, but most of our conversations were about things and ideas, not feelings. Heidi had a deep reserve and quietness so that I both trusted her and felt a little distance. My inner work was so pressing that I wanted to be able to broach it with her. And perhaps I sensed a little a more opening than before.

"I'm doing some really hard work in therapy now, about being sexually abused when I was a child."

"Oh?"

"Yeah. I don't remember it clearly, but I know it happened, it was my father, and I was little."

"Oh, that's harsh. I'm sorry you had to go through that."

"I've been working with these memories for several years now and sometimes it's really intense." I continued talking about the abuse but in a limited way, just testing the waters.

"I have a bit of a background, too," she said, and then, after a short silence, changed the subject. *Did I just hear what I thought I heard? Oh, my. Well, we'll have to come back to this later.*

Gradually, over time, Heidi and I began to share more deeply. It was comforting to have a friend who had also survived sexual abuse by her family. At the same time, with my other friend Helen, I could share my feelings in very raw and direct ways, telling her how my little girl felt. I was beginning to have a stronger network of friends.

I Xeroxed copies of the photograph of me when I was four, the one that looked like a sad refugee girl. One evening I carefully cut away the background and pasted the sad, blurry little girl into my drawing book. On sudden impulse, I drew next to her an orange glowing girl with open arms.

The next time I saw Sarah I told her, "I've been thinking about joy and openness. It's wonderful but it frightens me. I don't know if I want to go there. Why is it scary?" I showed her several pictures of little girls in bright colors with open arms and light around them.

"Oh, I love those colorful little ones!"

"But why do I feel scared?" I asked.

"I believe we come into the world in the open ecstatic state, every one of us. When a child is violated, this closes her down. She learns that it's dangerous to be open."

"Ah. Openness means danger. Yes, it feels that way."

"We need to open it up bit by bit," she said.

≈ 30 Almost Grace

ON A BRIGHT JULY afternoon with the breeze coming in through the dining room windows, we decorated the dining room with crepe paper streamers and balloons. Kathy and I twisted the streamers, Will tacked balloons in the high corners, and Suzie helped and chuckled to herself. There were seven of us for the birthday dinner, including Kathy's husband and step-daughter, and of course Myra at the head of the table for her eighty-seventh birthday.

The long family-heirloom table was laid with placemats and silver, a bouquet of daisies at the center. I'd made an angel food cake at home the day before, which we served with strawberries and whipped cream, and candles, of course.

Myra was very tired and pale but she seemed to relax and enjoy the proceedings more than usual. She sat at her end of the table with a soft smile on her face as she watched the generations interact and ask about one another's lives.

Two days later, I got a phone call at work. Kathy said, "I'm calling from St. Michael's hospital."

"What?"

"Yeah. Myra gave in and let me take her to her doctor for a check-up for her tiredness and breathlessness. Her doctor took one look at her and said, 'You're going to the emergency room. Now. You've got severe anemia and you need a transfusion immediately.'"

"Oh my God."

"Well you know Myra—she tried to argue about it, said she'd go home and think it over, but between the doctor and me, we got her to go. She wouldn't allow the ambulance, though. I drove her. She's getting the first transfusion right now and they want to keep her."

"OK, I'm coming down. Do I have time to go home and get clothes?"

"Oh yes, that's fine. I can handle it but if you want to come that would be great." Kathy was wonderful with medical emergencies. She was a vigorous advocate and go-between. I'd already seen her in action when my father was ill and when Suzie had been in the hospital.

I drove home, packed some clothes and my journal, and arranged for my neighbor to take care of the cats for an indefinite period.

When I arrived at the hospital, Myra and Kathy were still in the emergency unit. Myra looked tiny in the high hospital bed. She greeted me with a vague and slightly frightened smile. "You didn't have to come down. I'll be OK," she said.

"I want to be here. What did they say is wrong?"

"They suspect internal bleeding," Kathy answered. "They want her to stay both for the transfusions and for tests."

"I don't want tests," Myra said. "If it's my time to go, I'd rather go quietly."

"Well, let's see how it goes." We waited to do the arguing later.

The next day at the hospital, Myra was still insisting that she wanted to go home. The doctors wanted to do a colonoscopy to look for colon cancer. "I just want to die in peace."

"But Myra, you remember the thing about hospice. You can't get hospice care unless you have a diagnosis and a prognosis of less than six months," I said. We had learned about hospice care when Jack was dying. We were all upset that he could not benefit from hospice because the Parkinson's was such a long-term illness that there never came a time when the doctor could say that he had only six months to live. Myra had repeatedly told me,

"That sounds so wonderful, what they do. When it's my time, I want that."

"I just don't want to go through procedures that are useless. I'm not going to have surgery or radiation or any of that."

"We know that, and it's totally up to you about any treatment," said Kathy, "but you know the thing about hospice."

I quickly added, "Would you do it for us, so we can get help caring for you?" Finally, this caused her to agree.

The colonoscopy (not a fun procedure for anyone, especially a frail anemic old woman) showed that she had cancer. A young surgeon tried to persuade her to have surgery. "It's just like a glorified appendectomy," he said. That was supposed to be a selling point.

"No," she said, looking dignified despite her green hospital Johnny. "I don't think so."

"You know the cancer will progress and it will kill you," he said, frowning.

"I know that," she said tartly.

In another day or two we brought Myra home. Her personal physician shook her head in frustration and respect. She prescribed iron pills so that Myra's body could make more red blood cells. The doctors said that the cancer would spread and might shut down her liver or obstruct her bowel, either of which would be a painful way to die.

We helped her up the front steps. She sighed as she crossed the threshold into the hall, "What a relief to be home." For us, the work was just beginning. Kathy shopped for groceries while I changed the beds and made lunch. I stayed several more days to make sure Myra could make do on her own.

In the morning and evening I spent time in my own room at the top of the house. Parts of me were furious and scared.

> *Kathy and I are stretched so thin we are nearly invisible. We are trying to create a space in which Myra may feel safe to begin to have feelings and to give her own answers to questions. But meanwhile we are only the holders. Our feelings are not manifest, not asked for, not wanted.*

I CRAWLED OUT onto the studio floor, gradually sensing my weight on my hands and feet. I began to feel my own life around me—

friends, work, dance, nature. "It's such a relief to be home," I said to Sarah, unconsciously echoing Myra's thoughts.

"Yes, I bet. You have been spending a lot of time with Myra."

"I'm being patient and listening a lot, even though she doesn't say much. I'm tired of it. It's very hard work talking with Myra because I have to be so careful not to scare her back into her shell."

"How do you mean?"

"Well, if I ask her about anything significant, she goes quiet and I have to wait a long time until she might be ready to say what she's thinking. Or she might change the subject."

"She's not used to talking about the big stuff."

"No.... You know, Little Jane doesn't seem to be scared about Myra dying."

"Well remember," Sarah said, "you never had very much of her. Maybe it just won't be scary."

"I need a real mommy," I said, and snuggled next to her.

Sarah said, "It's up to Myra if she wants to understand more or think about things. hospice may provide some counseling or philosophy."

"We'll see."

"People tend to die as they live. My mother did that, she died the way she lived."

"How was that?" I asked.

"She didn't say 'I love you.' She didn't say her feelings."

"At least Myra says 'I love you' and 'thank you,' even if she has a lot of limits. She has a lot of limits, even though she says 'I love you.'"

THE CAMPGROUND WAS a tiny family-run place on a hillside in Vermont, quiet and remote. I had scheduled to go away on vacation at the end of July, but how could I leave in the middle of this crisis? Myra told me firmly, "Go ahead, take your vacation. I'll just be here. Don't worry about it." Kathy said the same. "You really need the vacation, and who knows how long this will go on." So I went.

I set up a spacious tent by the picnic table at my campsite. It rained. I spent long hours in the tent reading, drawing and writing. The drawings were unformed splotches of color.

Is Myra scared? Am I scared of her leaving or only about how we get from here to there? I imagine inability to do for herself, stubbornness, agencies, paperwork, phone calls, emergencies and reprieves.

Does Myra want more? Does she want to review her life? For her to go in peace, does that mean stirring up these questions, or letting the questions go? If I were dying I'd want to ask the questions, but for her, it might be enough to have her own way for once.

It was a vacation of many tears, but a very good time to listen to Little Jane. She needed empty space.

On one day of perfect weather, I climbed Mount Ellen, beginning when the sun slanted down the slope, lighting up tiny stalks of native purple orchids. During the long climb uphill I saw not a soul. The air at the top was cool, sunny, and crisp. A special ecological zone decorated the ridge—starry club moss, short balsam firs, corn lily with its blue berries, oxalis like shamrocks, and families of mushrooms. A fairyland repeated over and over, the growing things just being themselves, their cycle of life and death always the same and never the same.

"I DREAMED ABOUT a small furious animal," I told Sarah back in the studio. "It whirls. Nobody can handle it. It's dangerous. I have no idea what it means."

"Why don't you try being that animal?"

I snarled and raged around the space, baring my teeth and feeling very destructive. I was ready to shred anything in sight. Then I felt lost.

Sarah said, "Stick with the anger." I raged some more.

"I still don't get it, though. I can enter into it but I don't get it."

"Are you ready to hear a thought I have?"

"Not yet." I stayed non-verbal for a few more minutes. Then, "Yes, now I want to hear."

"I suspect it's your anger about not getting what you needed from Myra when you were little. And now she's leaving and you'll never get that from her."

"What? Oh... I see. Not only that but she's taking all the good attention with her. She's slurping up all the attention in the family.

We try and try to listen to Myra. She gets all the good energy. And my little girl is still deprived."

"That does heighten it."

"Can I do this? Be furious in one part and also be taking care and even be calm in another? I think I can."

"You already are doing it."

MYRA'S RED BLOOD COUNT was down again by mid-August, the transfused blood being lost from her system. Her doctor guessed that she had six to eight weeks to live. Myra herself was a little more doubtful. "If the iron kicks in, I could still be here in a year." She didn't seem too pleased about that prospect.

When the hospice nurse arrived for the first time, Kathy and Will and I were there, tensely sitting in the living room. We wanted to know how much care they would support.

"You have to understand. We don't provide round-the-clock care. If she needs that, you need to find somebody yourself." *Lots of luck getting Myra to accept having someone in the house,* I thought. "We can send somebody in twice a week to help with cleaning and household things."

"I don't need that now," Myra said.

"But we need you to get some help," I said. "We can't do it all."

"I don't want anybody yet. Maybe later. I'll be all right."

In the kitchen after the nurse left, Kathy and I looked at one another with tears in our eyes. "How are we going to get through this?" she asked.

"I don't know," I said, and we hugged one another tightly.

As soon as we walked back into the living room, Myra met us with a list of things to do. "I want you to look at my financial records and make sure you understand where everything is. I really think the two of you should split the family silver and take it away so it will be safe. If I go into the hospice facility, you'll need to put a burglar alarm on the house. And the two of you need to start making an inventory and deciding how all the family stuff is going to be divided." Her tone was cheerful and firm. *But I have some feelings about this—what about feelings?*

"I don't want Suzie to know that I'm sick. She's dealing with enough already. She can find out after it's over."

Kathy and I glanced at one another. "Uh, no. I don't think so," I said. "She really needs to know about this. Remember when Jack died? She did OK with it."

"Well, all right, if you must." We arranged to have Suzie visit two weeks later.

She's doing it again! Making it impossible to talk about feelings. I am furious. She's robbing us of this amazing, unique, once-in-a-lifetime opportunity. The same old stuff in a new context— she wants us to keep a conspiracy of silence.

Almost every weekend I went back to visit Myra. "You can ask me anything," she said one time. *Can I ? Can I really ask about the abuse? Do I want to? I'm afraid I could damage the trust I'm working to build. And I could meet denial, too. That would be hugely difficult.*

In the kitchen one morning I said, "I wonder if any particular memories come up for you?"

"No, nothing..." She said in a small voice, looking distantly out the window, clearly remembering something. "No, nothing in particular." There was a long silence.

"One thing I wonder about is Jack's contradictions. He had all these ideals of equality and yet he behaved strangely about women with all his affairs and that."

"He never listened to me. Well, I mean he never took my views into account. He would let me talk, but he wouldn't listen."

"Like about things at the shop?"

"About the shop, about money—he just wouldn't listen to me! There was the time he nearly got conned by some man who wanted him to invest all our savings in a scheme. Jack had the piece of paper and he had actually signed it, but I finally got it away from him. We hardly had any money then and it was just a hare-brained scheme! He was so gullible."

"If times had been different, would you have stayed with Jack?"

"I don't know," she sighed. "Maybe if we had understood more about how men and women are different..."

"How?" She replied with some things she heard from her favorite radio psychologist.

"Yeah," I said, "that's a lot of why I got divorced. He couldn't talk about feelings and it drove me nuts."

This is as close as I can get. My patience pays off in small coins. I push a little and listen a lot.

When I told Sarah about that conversation, she understood my feelings about the great gaping silences. She said, "I think on some soul level, she is touched by your attempts even if she often can't respond."

I wept, then said, "Little Jane is angry because Myra never was there and now she's leaving."

Sarah said, "I'm not going away and it's OK to need me a lot right now. And you know, you've already given Myra a lot. You've been her steadiest and safest person, and probably the greatest love of her life."

I cried and wailed, the whole front of my body hurting. "I've already done that, haven't I? I see that my little girl is already loving and generous. I don't know why she's so convinced that she's not. Just being there is a lot."

I felt a stirring inside and paused to listen, then said, "My little girl wants to ask—is it really OK to go beyond Myra? Is it OK to have so much creativity and strength and joy?"

"Yes it is, and I believe she would wish that for you," Sarah said.

"Oh, god, I wonder what it would be like to be saying goodbye to someone who could cry and say, 'I don't want to go' or 'I've had a full life'? Someone who could be present with me? I hope I can say a few things to her."

"You've already told her the things you appreciate about her."

"I keep wishing for more. My little girl wants to love Myra with an open heart. But it's not possible—she's not open to that. It's very sad. Especially sad because her heart isn't too small from meanness. She's not mean, she's scared. So very scared."

"It's hard to be open when the other person is closed."

"I feel shy about this. Is it OK to love you so much, Sarah? To feel such gladness just seeing your face? It's easy to love you. Is it OK?

She said, "It's part of the process. It's really OK. And if you depend on me you can let go of more of your expectations of Myra, things she could not give when you were little and will never be able to give. If you let go of those, you have more chance to be with her the way she is. And you know what an enormous gift that is, to have someone be with you as you are."

"But I guess not everybody you work with wants you to be their mommy. I mean, it's not like you encouraged me to go there."

"It's different for different people. You're right that not everybody uses the transference so much. And I'm honored that I can be in this position in your life."

"It doesn't scare you when I love you so much?"

"Not at all. I'm not going to run away. I can see how it makes you very vulnerable." She seemed to take it all in stride.

"I wonder if I want to ask Myra about the abuse. No, I mean not ask, but tell her. My memories are not negotiable."

"I wonder why you would want to tell?"

I paused to think. "To satisfy the little girl, I think. It's not for Myra."

"What would the little girl want from her, I wonder. What would she want from Myra?"

"She wants to be seen and heard. She wants Myra to say it's not fair, it should not have happened. She wants Myra to really feel how awful it was." I sighed. "Oh I see, what the little girl wants is not very likely at all to happen. I guess my little girl needs to get her goodies elsewhere. I guess I won't tell her. I'm not sure."

WE WERE SITTING in the living room in the fading daylight when I asked Myra what was the happiest time in her life. She surprised me by responding without a moment's hesitation, "The summer after we were married. We rented a cottage on the Maryland shore."

"And maybe you rented a boat," I said. "I remember pictures of that." I remembered another old snapshot, of Jack holding Myra in his arms and playfully threatening to drop her in the water, both of them smiling, looking impossibly young and happy.

Both of them were involved in politics when they married. "We had a circle of socialist friends who got together to talk and sing. We really believed in it," she sighed. "That was when Jack was doing union organizing in the steel mills."

"Secretly, right?" I asked.

"Yes. We stayed in Maryland for three years or so. Then we moved to Louisville in 1940 for his job with DuPont. Jack hated it, just hated it, and we were afraid his politics would be discovered. We had moved away from our friends. And Suzie was born soon after."

I pictured how isolated she had been. Myra paused, then said, "I had no idea about babies."

"Yeah, I bet. Your family wasn't the kind where people passed around babies and got together all the time." I hesitated, then ventured, "Aunt Virginia sent me the letters about Suzie a few years ago, the letters that you wrote her right after Suzie was diagnosed. That must have been a really hard time for you." This was not something Myra ever talked about, except recently she had wondered aloud whether she should have kept Suzie at home.

"I think you did really well to keep her with you for three years," I reassured her. "I know from the letters that the doctors wanted you to institutionalize her away right away."

"We didn't find that wonderful school till then. The other places sounded horrible, and we saw a few of them. They were."

"And I think you did the right thing to send her to that school. There was no support back then for keeping kids like that at home. How were Suzie and I together? I only have the vaguest memories."

"You didn't interact that much," she said. "Little Suzie slept most of the time."

I was remembering hugs and a presence. I didn't contradict her, but I mourned the gulf between us.

This was more sharing than I had ever had from Myra. Yet it felt tiny on the whole scale of intimacy.

The weekend arrived when we were to tell Suzie. I drove to get her. As I led her slowly up Myra's front steps, she wheezed from the effort and her hand was shaking in mine. Her Down syndrome was aging her rapidly and I suddenly was gripped by the thought that we could lose her soon, as well.

We walked into the living room where Kathy and Myra were already sitting. I sat next to Suzie on the couch by the window. After a few awkward pleasantries, I said to Suzie, "Myra is getting tired."

"I know." Suzie glanced at Myra, who nodded at her.

"She'll be sleeping more and more. The doctor told her she's sick and she'll be getting more tired."

"Yes," she said, her eyes drifting downwards. I took her hand.

"Do you remember how Jack got very tired and was in bed a lot?"

"Uh-huh." Suzie got very quiet and sad.

"Myra's getting very tired like that." Suzie kept her eyes down and wouldn't say anything more. I knew she had heard the message.

"I didn't think I'd still be here. The iron seems to be working," Myra said on the phone in late October. She continually surprised me by talking openly about her death. "I wonder when I should stop taking the iron. I don't want the cancer to spread and get to the painful stage." I thought that the waiting was driving her crazy, too.

"I can stop any time," she said.

"Yes, it's entirely up to you to choose." She might have more sense of control than any time in her life, I thought.

Then I told Myra about a student who had been paralyzed in an accident and was writing about his disability. She instantly said, "Oh, it's a bad idea to study it. So many things are solved by not thinking about them." That would be a terrific epitaph, I thought.

Now that she was feeling better, she acted more distant, just like her old self. When I visited, she made sure I was busy every moment.

The prospect of death is wonderfully clarifying. When Myra's better, she's worse—anxious, picky, interfering, busy, busy.

When I saw Sarah I told her about Myra's improvement and her distance, how angry it made me.

"Sarah, would you talk directly to Little Jane about this? Myra wasn't there for me then and she's not there now."

Sarah said, "Little one, it's hard to understand because Myra was a grownup when you were little, but some grownups aren't big, they're scared and small and can't deal with feelings. You tried again and again but Myra can't be there."

"She's a sad person," I said in Little Jane's voice.

"Yes, she is sad."

The months dragged on. As Kathy and I juggled our full-time jobs and the extra responsibility, something had to give. I said no to several conferences and canceled my out-of-town trips. I see now that this passage gave me the gift of loosening my ties to the professional world. I never went back to the same all-out pace.

One morning at work a student asked me for an extra meeting on a Friday. "I can't," I said. "I'm just flat out with my mother's needs."

She laughed, startling me, then explained. "It's all right. I really respect how you are trying to keep space for your mother's dying. I laughed because it's a good role model the way you said no to me."

"Thanks for understanding." I smiled at her with tears in my eyes.

In a seminar class, I told the students that my mother was dying and that I didn't have the energy I usually had. It was sometimes hard just preparing for class. They volunteered to take on more of the responsibility, and I was I glad I had leaned on them.

Christmas came and went. It was a desolate holiday. I had the impression Myra wished she didn't have to engage in it.

"I THINK MYRA IS slipping," I said to Kathy on the phone about nine months after the diagnosis. "She told me she is losing her appetite. She said she has to plan when to get up and walk across the room."

"Oh my," Kathy said. "Yes, I've seen it too. She has no energy. But she still said no when I asked her if we could get a hospice volunteer in to do some cleaning or cooking."

"Do you think she will want us around to help?"

"I bet she won't. You remember when she was in the intensive care unit with that pacemaker emergency?"

"Yeah?"

"She was on a respirator so she couldn't talk. She scribbled on the bedsheet, 'GO AWAY.'"

"Oh, wow. You never told me. Poor you," I said. "I'm so glad that we are together on this."

"Me, too, Sis. I don't know how I'd do it without you."

About a week later, Myra convened a conference with Kathy and me and the hospice nurse. The nurse, who had been visiting Myra weekly, was very admiring of her toughness in getting through all of this on her own. She said, "It's difficult not knowing what will happen. But you're still getting something out of life. You're interacting with people."

Myra was silent.

"You don't want to go by bowel obstruction if you have a choice," the nurse offered next.

"Yes," Myra said. "I really don't want that. And I have no energy. I can't see, either."

The nurse suggested more household help, and Myra allowed her to schedule a volunteer for a few hours a week of housework.

Kathy asked, "Do you want to be here at home and have us care for you? We are willing to do it."

"No, I'd like to go to the hospice facility. You know I've dreamed of that. I think it's time—I'm going to quit the iron pills."

The nurse looked at Kathy and at me. We both nodded with tears in our eyes. "We're with her in whatever she decides to do," Kathy said.

A few days later, Myra was on the phone. "I've been wondering whether I should tell Shirley across the street." Shirley was her only friend. I was stunned, but on reflection not surprised.

"Well, what have you told her?"

"Not much. I told her about the anemia, but she doesn't know about the cancer. I don't want her breaking down in front of me. I've gotten some kind of equilibrium and I don't want her to disturb it."

"If anybody's entitled to cry," I said, "I think it's family before Shirley. And Kathy and I have been careful not to."

"You've been great," she said. "That person they got me for housework, Margie, asked me if I ever cried about it. I said no. She said, 'You should, you should cry.' I don't want to go into it. I'm doing OK the way I am. I want to keep Margie busy. I'm going to tell her I don't want to talk about it."

"I think it's up to you," I said, feeling a peculiar mix of indignation at this Margie's presumption, pride about Myra's toughness and frustration at her closedness. "It's so odd, the whole thing hardly seems real to me."

"It doesn't seem real to me either."

"I love you, Myra."

"I love you, too, sweetie, very much."

The next week when I visited, I brought Suzie for the last time. Myra told her directly, "I'm very proud of you," and she meant it.

Suzie smiled and looked shyly down at her hands. The rest of the time she was solemn and quiet.

THE FOLLOWING WEDNESDAY the phone rang at work. It was Kathy, and my heart pounded. "Myra called me this morning to tell me she was too tired, and it was time to go to the hospice place. I went and got her right away. When I helped Myra walk away from the house, she turned and said, 'Goodbye, house.'"

"Oh, that is so sad!"

"But she seems happy to be at hospice. She said, 'Now I can really relax.'"

"That's amazing."

I packed my things and drove down, after finding substitute teachers for my classes and letting my colleagues know that I was away for the duration. Will arrived the following day. We visited her in the quiet, airy hospice house.

At first Myra was totally conscious—weak but very alert. She kept hold of all her marbles.

I was there when Myra spoke to her sister Virginia on the hospice phone for the last time. I dialed the number and handed her the receiver. She told Virginia, "They are taking great care of me. This is not so bad."

When Myra got tired, she told us to go away. Will and I went hiking in the April woods at a state park. After about an hour I told him to go on. I slept peacefully under the budding trees by a swamp in the sun while he hiked on.

In a couple of days, Myra became exhausted. She let me feed her for the very first time. She only wanted the dessert, a peach shortcake. It broke my heart, the trusting way she opened her mouth for the spoon.

I tried to take her hand while she was awake but she quietly pulled it away. The next day she started slipping out of consciousness and then I could hold her hand. I stayed there for some hours, listening to her labored breathing, looking at her frail body, remembering scenes of our life together, and crying from time to time.

Six days after Myra went into the hospice facility, the phone rang at 6:30 AM at Myra's house where Will and I were staying. I knew immediately. "She's gone," Kathy said. "She slipped away with no one there, just as she would have wished."

≈ 31 Down the Labyrinth

I DREAM I AM hiking down Mount Rainer, back to the parking lot. It's the end of the day. The little girl who is with me runs ahead towards the car. She wants me to throw her the keys. I don't want to throw the keys to her because they might get lost in the bushes. She wants to run and start the red car.

This dream felt urgent. The key to something. It was six months after Myra died, and I had recently stopped seeing Sarah in the studio, since I felt that talk therapy was doing the job, but I called and she agreed to meet in the studio for this particular session.

I told her the dream, then walked out on the studio floor. I felt myself as the dreamer, keys in hand, wondering whether to toss them to the eager girl ahead of me.

"No," I said out loud, "I need to give the keys to Silent Girl instead." My mood downshifted into a lower gear. Silent Girl had recently appeared in my life. She'd first shown up when I was frustrated with my physician and could not bring myself to confront her. I clammed up, feeling an old helplessness. When I talked to Sarah about the incident and she tried to help me speak, I instead got more and more stubbornly silent. I felt possessed by a little girl whose only power was in keeping her mouth shut.

I sensed myself handing the car keys to Silent Girl, then being in her body, slowly walking forward, keys in my right hand. I began to move in a spiral, circling towards the right. My left hand found a rough, damp stone wall. With my eyes closed, I saw its dark red color. I followed this spiral down, down into the earth, circling towards something important.

After a space of fifteen minutes, I came back to the present reality and sat beside Sarah. I told her the sensations and images. "I think Silent Girl is leading me deeper, down to a dark place. It feels like a labyrinth—not a twisting one, but a necessary, ceremonial one."

"The change was dramatic," she said. "I agree that you should listen to Silent Girl. And can I say something else?"

"Sure."

"I think that dream is also telling you not to give up the keys to that Eager Girl, the one who wants to go full speed ahead. She's too young to drive."

"I know who you mean," I chuckled, "the one who always says, 'Go for it! Right now!'"

"Mmm-hmm. Slowness is a virtue, too."

My mouth was full of silence, but it was my turn to talk. Ten of us were sitting on the floor in a circle in a dim old carriage house—eight women participants and two leaders. It was the second weekend of our Authentic Movement advanced training course that would meet for six long weekends in a year. I glanced around, feeling the compassion of one, the curiosity of another, the puzzlement of a third, the patience of the leaders.

With pounding heart, I sat quiet for half a minute and then said, "I have a very silent little girl inside of me. Sometimes she won't speak at all, but I know she's an important, deep part of me. I hope you'll bear with me when I need to be quiet. And I need a lot of alone time, too, even in these weekends together."

Respect and care glistened in their faces. One woman said, "I look forward to knowing why she needed to go silent." It felt safe to trust them with the mystery I was holding. In our movement sessions, I had many opportunities to embody this silent girl, huddling in the corner or walking slow spirals into darkness.

Content

No container could hold me
yet I am held.
Impossibly, all of me
by people who do not know me
each imperfect and yet
my head is held
my silence is heard
my power is felt, my heart is eased.
The magic holds.
I feel the threads held taut
by all these hands
and it is my work to go forth in faith.
doing the work that is mine alone
and not alone, for all of us.

This group witnessed all the years of my writing. After our training was completed, we formed a peer group that still convenes for two long weekends every year. With our different gifts of sociability and silence, laughter and depth, we support one another's journeys.

ROCKETING ALONG THE Wilbur Cross Parkway towards New York City, I scarcely noticed the bare dogwoods and dry grasses or the Depression-era bridges with their individual facades highlighted by the slanting sun. It was the day before Thanksgiving 2001, six months after Myra's death, and I was headed for my son's apartment to celebrate the holiday with an assortment of his friends.

A fire of joy kindled in my chest as I drove and mused on the work I had been doing in therapy. It was six years since I'd begun this unexpected journey. Suddenly it came to me, *I could write a book about my journey of healing.*

I shouted *Yes!* at the windshield. I could honor the beauty I felt in the work as well as Sarah's loving, insightful support. A story like this could be of use to others. Animated by this vision, I talked out loud to myself for a few miles until I spotted one of those dinky gas-station convenience stores sprinkled by the highway near New York. Diving into a parking space, I grabbed my journal from the front seat and began scribbling. I immediately knew that the memoir would start with that first memory of the pain between my legs.

I still don't understand the paradox, why the impulse to tell my story came exactly when I was paralyzed by silence. It makes sense, but not logically.

MEANWHILE SILENT GIRL kept hanging around, defying Sarah and me to get close to her. She'd show up in therapy sessions and refuse to speak, just sitting there with her arms crossed, mouth clamped shut.

"Sarah?" I said one day.

"Uh-huh?" Her brown eyes glinted with interest.

"I think I need to go down in the labyrinth to find that silent girl. She's like Lost Girl all over again, but... it's like she's both hiding and insisting I come find her."

"I see. She's been baffling me. Can I help at all?"

"Would you sit here next to me so I'm not alone?"

"Sure," and she crossed over to the couch and sat close beside me. I took her hand and she held mine firmly.

"I see the landscape. It's in the Southwest—open and dry. It's near sunset and I am walking." The images came to me and I let them unfold.

"Now I'm getting closer to the labyrinth. Here it is, opening downwards in the earth." I saw and felt it vividly. The walkway was wide enough for one person. I moved forward on the packed dirt, a damp wall curving on my left. There was a mud parapet on my right, about hip-high. "When I look down, I can't see anything and I feel dizzy."

"OK, take your time."

"I'm walking down. Oh, now there's a big bat-creature overhead—it's screaming at me that I shouldn't be doing this. It's scary."

"Keep breathing."

I breathed in and out. "I'm going to keep on in spite of it. Another ugly creature like a toad is there. It says I'm too slow, not getting anywhere. But I'm still walking."

"Good. I'm here."

"Down, down, around." In my mind it's getting darker, walking slowly down. "Now it's foggy. I can't see anything." I gripped Sarah's hand. "Nothing at all. I'm sure there's nothing there to be seen. I should just give up." I felt a blankness of despair.

Sarah squeezed my hand.

"I'm keeping on. Now I'm down at the bottom and it's just big paving blocks, red stone blocks. I don't see any little girl."

"Maybe she's hiding."

Tears came. "I think there are cracks between the paving stones and I think she's underneath."

"Can you call her?"

"I'm trying to talk to her but nobody answers. She might be scared." I stayed with that image, calling and listening.

"I'm afraid our time is nearly up."

"All right. Maybe I can leave a note for her even though I can't see her." In my mind I wrote "I will be back" on a slip of paper and slipped it through the cracks in the stones. Then I slowly trudged up the spiral, emerging into the sunset at the top.

"What do I do with this?" I asked.

"Give it time. You might need to revisit her many times."

"But if she won't respond at all…?"

"Just be patient. She needs you."

A few weeks later, I sat on the couch and asked Sarah to sit close beside me. "OK, I'm ready to start," I sighed. "Even before I go there, I feel so much heaviness. I feel the terrible fullness in my mouth, a lot of silence and darkness."

"I'm here. I can't be right where you are, but I'm close by."

I closed my eyes. "I'm walking down slowly. It's very dark and I'm scared. Now I come to the fog and a demon is saying there's nothing there, nothing there."

"You can talk back to it."

"Get back, you demon! I know there's a little girl there and I need to reach her," I said loudly. I took a deep breath. "Now I'm at the bottom. It's very dry and cold. There are the paving stones with cracks between. Now there is a stone wall and a window with bars. Darkness beyond it. I can't find a little girl who should be here. I can't find her and I'm really scared."

"Why is that?"

"I am terrified of finding her and not being able to hold all her feelings. And I'm supposed to be the big one. She's so little and *she* held all those secrets." I blew out a breath, feeling deep shame weighting my heart. "At the same time I'm frightened that I'll never find a little girl. I can't see her. Where is she? Is there anyone here at all? I need to write her a note." Very slowly I wrote on my leg with my index finger, *I want to find you*. That's all I could write. I was ashamed again that I couldn't write that I wanted to hear her or offer her encouragement.

I asked Sarah to help me get back. She held my hand and said, "Remember the way. Walk, one foot after another. Breathe." Gradually I could feel myself moving away from the depths. When I saw myself emerging in the desert there were colors! Deep blue, yellow at the sky's edge, stars above.

In the dark of winter, Silent Girl was with me every day. I felt that she was holding things I couldn't bear to see. Yet every day I held her and her silence.

> *There are a lot of reasons why little girls need to be silent. To keep secrets in order to survive. Because of the unbearable, unspeakable things happening in their mouths. Stubbornly, to resist being forced to speak. I have so much need to be silent.*

As I came closer to this girl, I fell into the pit of silence. When I was in therapy, I could feel myself merged with the silent girl. "Sarah, I just want to stay in the darkness. The Silent Girl wants me with her completely."

"You really need not to do that. It's not good to stay with her only. You have to shuttle back and forth."

"Silent Girl is frustrated with this. She wants me to be right there with her."

"I see that she does, but you need a little separation."

"I don't understand. I don't see how to do that and also be with her. I feel stuck."

"I hear you, but stay with the stuckness. It will get resolved, I trust. It's important to understand Silent Girl but do it safely."

I did not see how that was possible.

At our next session I felt the silent girl inside me. I sat with arms crossed, stubborn and hopeless.

Sarah said from her chair a few feet away, "I don't know how to relate to her sometimes. It's frustrating. I don't know how to help." A slight edge of sharpness in her voice scared me.

A voice burst out of my mouth. "Nobody's going to help me. Nobody's here. Nobody will ever be here. Nobody will ever understand. They don't want to come here. Nobody ever will. It's hopeless. There is nobody. I'm all alone." I felt tension from head to toe.

There was silence in the small office. "Wow, she spoke," I said.

"Yes, I heard that."

"She was desperate."

"Mmm-hmm."

I sat on the floor and began slowly to inch towards Sarah. She held my head and shoulders in her lap. For a few minutes, the silent girl was not alone.

≈ 32 Beginning

I FEEL THE EARTHQUAKE sensation of creating my own world—a world of truth apart from the one I grew up with, a world of values and priorities apart from my work setting. An everyday world of going towards what I love, following the feeling of rightness. No wonder it feels big and disorienting!

Writing my story opened up new realms of creativity and new paths to recovery. First I had to carve out the time. Luckily I had a sabbatical coming, which I eagerly dedicated to beginning the memoir. I was close to retirement anyway and figured I could get away with a minimum of professional work.

Each time I started a new section of the memoir, I opened my old journals and sketchbooks and the feelings came pouring out—intertwined, confusing, repetitive. Mistrust arose in my daily life when I was writing about mistrust, anger when I wrote of anger. Finding my own method to bring them to order and expression was a wild gallop into claiming my creative life.

The first third of the book came through me rapidly, but then I bogged down in something sticky.

"Sarah," I said into the quiet of her office, the cricket chirps of late summer filtering in through the open windows, "I'm feeling stuck. Why am I doing this all over again?"

"Stuck where?" Sarah asked.

"With the void and rage and trying to tell Myra. I'm still that little girl trying, trying and she won't listen. I don't have the words, I can't make it clear. Myra questions me sharply. She doesn't hold me. She doesn't ask how I feel."

"How old do you think you were?"

"I don't know. Five or six. It feels like it's after he did the mouth stuff to me. And Myra says *forget it*. Maybe that means she actually believes me but what she says is to pretend it didn't happen… but it's all vague and not clear." I started to feel anxious and uncertain.

"I am with you," said Sarah. "Tell me where you feel it in your body."

I plunged in again headlong. "She says forget it. Everything is whirling black fog…. It's here in my chest." I put my palm to my breastbone and ribs. Breathing was difficult. "I am ripped from my own chest. I can't stay, I have to go. It hurts so much in my heart. This girl, the little one who is so *truthful*, she's sent away, all alone."

I noticed that my hands were stuck together, sweating palm to palm like my relationship with Myra. "The Jane who stays is the one who sticks to Myra and is loyal. She does the best she can to be a very Good Girl and to get whatever connection she can. She did amazingly well, in a way. Walking around like those figures in stories made of mud, no spirit. Being successful."

"Yes, you did that."

"The other part of me, right at that moment of Myra's denial she is lost. She has to go away. She can't stay because she knows the truth and she is hurting so much. She goes far, far away."

Sarah nodded with a sympathetic look in her eyes.

I gulped, a white-hot searing pain in my breastbone. "At the moment of the split, so much pain right here. I see my red, dripping heart being cut out. Half the little girl remains, half goes. It hurts unbearably."

"I know. Try and stay with that for a while if you can," Sarah said.

I stayed there. Gasping in pain and howling, grabbing Kleenex from the box beside me. In the moment of open-ribs bloody ripping apart. "It feels like what Jack did shook my soul loose inside me. Then when Myra would not listen and meet me, I really... the part of me that remembered the abuse had to leave. She became Silent Girl."

"Did you ever think Big Jane would come for you?"

"No, I didn't. I thought I'd be lost for ever. How amazing. She came!" My chest opened and my breathing slowed.

Later Sarah said, "I thought you'd need to come to this point."

"I knew something needed to move but I didn't know what. Oh god, that was really hard work. The pain was unbearable for Little Jane—the pain of betrayal, losing Myra, confusion of truth, lack of solid ground. I had to flee from that. But going caused pain, too. Huge tearing agony in my chest and heart. Heart ripped open."

"You did very good, hard work. I'm proud of you." She hugged me. "Remember, I'm around if you need to call."

It took a while to integrate this soul-knowledge. The academic year intervened. During vacations I wrote parts of the memoir.

On an August morning a year later, I sat in my rocking chair in the morning, talking with Little Jane and hearing the robins outside. I felt warm and expansive inside, appreciating the process of writing about finding that Lost Girl. A vivid image came suddenly and I rushed to my kitchen table to draw it.

Dark, vague gray clouds covered the right side of the page where Silent and Lost Girls lived. An ordinary square house on the left for Good Girl. But I saw something new. In the jagged red split between, there was a ray of light beaming off into outer space.

I showed Sarah my drawing of the split. "See, we knew about the Good Girl and Lost and Silent Girls, but there's this loving, innocent, open girl whirling away like an invisible particle. Leaving my heart."

"Yes. It's to do with soul," she said. "Always there but invisible."

"I feel like I'm going toward the light! What a miracle. Can this be real? Is it true that I don't have to live in the ugly, yucky, dark, lonely places any more?"

"There does come a time," Sarah said. "It can't be predicted, but it happens. You were willing to go into the dark for so long, and so deep."

"Yes, I was. This is all new. This little girl of light and love." I sighed and felt my chest expand, the air moving easily in. "I need

Remember

how it began
you were everywhere
in the trees, the rocks,
running through like a golden thread
seeping like water
no form only soul
delighting in all being,
then in your incarnated being
fingers, toes, belly, spit.
Remember how it began
offspring of the world
infinite, unbounded, confident
in your connection.
Soon enough you learned boundaries
and how it was to be violated.
Schoolbooks, grades, family fights,
starched dresses, silence,
cowboys and Indians,
secrets, rape.
Half a century later
you unlearned, pulling
the barbed strands
from the living flesh
weeping oceans to sail
home on, in the wind of change
to the harbor of arms,
small again, in the lap of acceptance.
Huge waves of love, a tempest.
Quiet now, can you accept the miraculous
ordinariness of being just a part
of it all—branches, chickadees,
laundry on the line, clouds, sleeping cats.

to get used to it, understand how to be, how to live differently. Things could be easy. Wow. How will it manifest in the world, I wonder?"

"You will see. But also, be careful with it and protect yourself. It's not about being all open all the time. You can notice how things really are and how people are and act accordingly."

"It seems paradoxical to be more open and need more protection."

"It is, but it is true." At the end of the session, Sarah said, "I need to tell you again, it is a privilege to be part of this process."

I really get to have all this? Really? Spirit and heart and words and light. Really, all this I've been asking for, looking for—it's not too much to ask?

My incredulous heart. I get to have all this. Love, belief, welcome, joy, fun. Wonder. Unknown, unbounded, loving, amazing grace. Inner work, writing, heart, connection.

The feelings of joy and lightness stayed with me for weeks. I remember visiting my son in New York. I sat on the subway newly amazed at all the people—the young Puerto Rican man slumped opposite me with his huge sneakers, baseball cap and bravado covering his feelings; the weary mother holding the hand of her pink-clad, bright-eyed little girl—each with a tender soul inside. I felt like a butterfly—fragile but sturdy and very light.

I wish the lightness were with me all the time. It's not, but I do have an embracing sense of loving all the aspects of myself—the gnarly, snarly ones as well as the happy and loving ones. Even that yearning to have it all be OK forever—on a good day I can see that it's just part of the package.

I am amazed at how different my life feels now. Writing this memoir not only gave me permission but actually forced me to carve a new life. It compelled me to live the life of an artist, paying attention to moods and subtle perceptions, writing in intense spurts of energy interspersed with apparently lazy days of vagueness, naps, hikes, and staring into space.

I didn't intend to become a writer. Over those years of recovery, as I sat at my kitchen table after work and covered acres of paper with my slanting, illegible scrawl, I let words emerge like creatures from the chaos of my subconscious. I learned to listen to the ones that spoke back to me, mirroring the turmoil.

The year my mother died, I joined a writing group and began to take my writing seriously. My flooding grief mixed with anger at her limited, timid life and poured into poems.

Art was a further stretch. It had been a forbidden area. When I was a kid, I was good at everything except art. Seeing my attempts at drawing, my mother laughed and said, "Well, you're no artist," and it stuck. In the anger and confusion that surged in me during recovery, I began drawing. When no words could touch the desolation and incredulous sting of betrayal, I would fist a black crayon and transfer its soul onto the page, adding jagged red, brown, purple slashes. I ground the colors onto the page until I felt a satisfaction of release inside—*That's it. That is really the way it feels.* Art was a place beyond judgment. Over and over, I assured myself *This is just for me, not for anyone to judge.* When my therapist said "This is really expressive—I hope someone else is seeing it," I brushed her comments aside.

But art-as-therapy gave birth to art-as-play. Now as I survey a canvas in progress, of course the critical voices sometimes hover nearby and whisper, *You have no idea what you are doing. What makes you think you can do this?* My pulse quickens but then I ask somewhere inside, *What's needed here? What color do you want to make? Oh, a bit of ochre in the ultramarine? What would that do? Let's try it!*

There's no one I need to please or impress with my art. It's deep play, improvising with color and form. I love to paint with the palette knife, because the added randomness of it is like dancing with a partner. I don't have control, I can only suggest and see what happens.

I love the solitude and connection to myself that the creative process has brought me. It's balanced by deep friendships and groups that I both cherish and take for granted—my dear writing group of kindred souls and my peer movement group that's stable and yet brings new excitement every week. I also have developed a clearer spiritual practice based on Buddhism.

My life is a rich weaving of the creative, spiritual, emotional, and intellectual. Some days are structured by movement or writing group meetings, while others are open to my sensing of what I desire to do. I always start the day by reading spiritual writing, sitting with my little girls, and journaling.

One sunny day in June 2004 I dropped my gardening tools and walked to the road to retrieve the mail from my mailbox. Among the bills and catalogs was a fat white envelope from the college. Opening it, I found documents describing a retirement buy-out offer from the college. To my own shock, my instant response was yes! In two semesters I said goodbye to students and colleagues and went into retirement. Although I enjoyed teaching right up through my last semester, when I left I did not glance back. Of course I would have retired at some point, but I doubt I would have approached the richness of the life I have now if I had not gone through the deep work of healing from trauma.

WHAT IS HEALING? Have I found it? It is the absence of negative symptoms—the flashbacks gone, the sense of wrongness about myself replaced by a general sense of rightness. I like where I am and who I am. The closed and fearful parts of me take less space.

I know where my weak spots are. I'll always be susceptible to the fear that people won't hear me or won't believe me. I notice when that feeling comes up and I can talk to Little Jane to let her know I hear the feeling and it's just a feeling. It may or may not be true that the particular person won't listen. These core issues are so familiar, they are almost like wild animals that have been tamed. Sometimes I can chuckle at them.

But healing is a lot more than the absence of bad feelings and patterns. It is the positive presence in my life of the joy and solidity that was my birthright. I think I am fortunate to be a person of natural enthusiasm and liveliness. Now these qualities are manifest in my many creative activities, my garden, and walks in nature.

Healing is a sense of connection and wholeness. It's not every moment that I feel connected to the world of people, trees, and clouds. Even the best mystics seem to get there only part of the time. Rumi, the Persian poet, is eloquent on the absence as well as the presence of "the Beloved"—his muse, love, and God. But I know it is possible and I am going in that direction.

Healing is feeling my story as beautiful despite all the pain and struggle.

Healing is watching my son grow into a man so like my father and so different. It is being open with him and letting him know how his actions affect me. It is being glad to see that he has learned to contain his anger and not poison others with it. There's something inexpressibly healing about having a man in my family line know the truth and support me in my journey, as Will has done.

Healing is choosing friends who celebrate my being. I have said goodbye to several friends who did not seem able to hear me or who took up all the space with their crises. I have moved away from others who are nice but not able to swim in the depths. Many of my same friends are still with me—Helen, Marianne, Heidi and others—and I've added a few close ones from the worlds of writing and dance.

Healing is a continual unfolding. It is not all done. Over time I feel more of my parents' love inside of me, while not denying their faults. I continue to gain insights into my life and family.

In the end, healing wasn't so much about making a clear story as about believing and trusting myself. It wasn't so much about reconciling with my parents for what they did, but more about reconciling with the many inner selves who lived to tell the tale.

"SARAH," I SAID TO HER recently, "things have shifted."

She looked at me expectantly.

"I mean.... I'm kind of shy of saying it, but you're not as magic to me as you were. I miss it, that huge love-feeling where I am so young and you are exactly my mommy. It's more like I take you for granted now."

"Well then," she chuckled, "I guess it worked the way it's supposed to."

"I still love you but it's not so very big. But what happens to the magic? I don't want it to go away."

"What do you think? Where is it?"

"Well, it's there in my connection to the little girls—sometimes I feel it really clearly in the morning when I sit with them. Sometimes I don't feel it as strongly."

"Um-hmm."

"And it comes through in other ways in my life... with my friends and how we share. In my writing, especially the memoir... and my poetry. And in dancing and connecting to other people through movement. And nature. And my drawing and painting. Sometimes I feel it, my own magic, sometimes it's more diffuse."

"I think you have a lot of that spirit. I see it," she said, her brown eyes twinkling.

I closed my eyes a minute and smiled through tears.

When I decided to see Sarah only once a week instead of the twice-a-week that had been my luxury for about five years, I told her, "My little girl is scared you won't be here for us."

"I'm always here," she said, "whether you see me once a week, twice a week, or not at all."

She spoke truth. Sarah's caring spirit is inside me, available when I need it, along with my own strong and tender Big Jane. If my little girls crave comforting when I sit with them in the morning, I hold them. I often go with them to that cabin in the woods where the spirit of Sarah lives. She is a beloved internal character who watches with love as I and the little girls dance into the future.

Ancient Fountain

To Sarah

The divine is like that in us.
Inexhaustibly fresh it pours
out of the broken statue
with its chipped nose, missing arm.
As a tired mother is
to her infant the very face of god
and the baby's need pulls
the immortal milk into her breast, you
were willing to be called
into service as the messenger,
or perhaps the incarnation. The ways

we embody love in this imperfect
world are baffling in their beauty and
their incompleteness. Yet you
were glad to make of yourself
the rough mask that my longing
could paint to perfection, so
my child-spirit could
fill it with wonder.

Stone by stone we built
the safe-enough temple
where this heart, again whole,
could for entire minutes
undamaged and radiant
accept its mission of tenderness.
Now you appear older,
more furrowed around the eyes,
still performing your sacred rites,
opening up the temple each morning.
When we meet at the wellhead,
each carrying her amphora,
I greet you and embrace you.

≈ Afterword

WHEN I WAS FIRST INSPIRED to write this memoir, I knew that I wanted to tell the story for people like me—abuse survivors with fragmentary memories—and also for anyone who is on a journey of self-discovery. I knew it was necessary to leave all the doubts and unclear places showing.

Once I started writing, I felt both blessed and cursed to have stacks of past journals—copious and overflowing with emotions. After each therapy session, I was in the habit of writing several pages of my immediate recollections of what had happened, including significant dialogue. This was for my own benefit, because I found it helped me to keep hold of the details. Otherwise, my memory could be watery. I also kept a daily journal. The journals have allowed me to reconstruct detailed scenes of what happened in therapy and elsewhere.

In striving to convey my truth, I have mostly stuck to the literal facts, to the best of my ability. However, I often compressed time by consolidating two or three therapy sessions into one, for the reader's sake. The indented italicized passages in the text are taken nearly verbatim from my journals of the relevant times.

I have changed the names of all the people and some details of persons and places to protect anonymity.

Numerous friends and writing groups encouraged me all along the line, from my first scribblings to the final edits. I cannot thank you enough, all of you who believed in me and in this project, and who gave me support, feedback, and love.

CPSIA information can be obtained
at www.ICGtesting.com
Printed in the USA
LVOW08s0932140617
538086LV00001B/35/P

9 780981 583020